OUR FALKLANDS WAR

THE MEN OF THE TASK FORCE
TELL *THEIR* STORY

GEOFFREY UNDERWOOD

MARITIME BOOKS
1983

£3.95

Credits

We are grateful to all those men and women who were interviewed for this book. Their personal testimony of long lonely days in the South Atlantic will no doubt be appreciated by all who read this book.

Without the excellent photographs—taken by both professional and amateur photographers only half the story could be told. Our thanks must be recorded to those who sailed in the Task Force.

Petty Officer (Phot) R. Birkett
Leading Airman (Phot) A. Campbell
Petty Officer (Phot) J. Fletcher
Petty Officer (Phot) P. Holdgate
Leading Airman (Phot) R. Ryan
Leading Airman (Phot) R. Toyer
Lieutenant R. Bell-Davies RN
Band Sgt R. Ireland
Lt Cdr R. Nichol RN

Commando Forces News Team
The Photographic Section
  HMS Hermes
  HMS Invincible
  HMS Fearless
  HMS Intrepid

We would also like to record photographic help received from:
The Directorate of Public Relations (RN)
Commander-in-Chief Fleet
Flag Officer Scotland & Northern Ireland
Flag Officer Portsmouth
Flag Officer Plymouth

  HMS Neptune
  HMS Heron
  HMS Seahawk

The Fleet Photographic Unit
H.M. Dockyard Devonport
Western Morning News Co Ltd

Contents

Author's notes

Many journalists, who sailed with the Task Force, have written books giving their own accounts of the Falklands campaign from its very beginnings to the surrender at Port Stanley.

My brief was to interview men from many of the ships and units when they returned home, recording their own very personal memories of the battle on land, at sea and in the air.

The cross-section of those interviewed over many weeks included soldiers, sailors, Royal Marines and a few of the women nurses, who sailed in the hospital ship, Uganda.

The men ranged from an 18-year-old Royal Marine, who lost his foot before he was old enough to vote, to the captains of ships and the officers who led units in the fierce fighting ashore.

This book is the personal story of just some of the Servicemen and civilians, who took part in the campaign 8,000 miles from home. But it is a tribute to them all, particularly those who did not come home.

Geoffrey Underwood.

Geoffrey Underwood.

Introduction

All Plymothians, and a great majority of West Countrymen, will know that a large proportion of the South Atlantic Task Force which retook the Falkland Islands and their dependencies in the winter (summer to you!) of 1982 had their bases and their homes in the South West. We who went South were very conscious of it too and I for one felt the connection very strongly; from the tremendous and energetic help we all received in early April; through the anxious days which followed, with the loss of West Country ships and men, and the great support given to all our families; the elation of the end of the fighting in mid June; the extraordinarily stirring reception, given I believe from a sense of sharing and rejoicing in an achievement of which we could all be proud, when men and ships returned home through July and August; and finally for me the moving Service on Plymouth Hoe, and the Remembrance of those who did not come back and the families who mourned them.

It is therefore entirely fitting that Geoffrey Underwood, who is both a West Country journalist, and a trusted and understanding friend to us in the Services, should have gathered together into a book the series of articles he wrote on the people and units whose home is in the area, and who played such a distinguished part in last year's stirring events.

I hope you will enjoy it.

Jeremy Moore

MAJOR GENERAL SIR JEREMY
MOORE KCB, OBE, MC*

FALKLAND ISLANDS

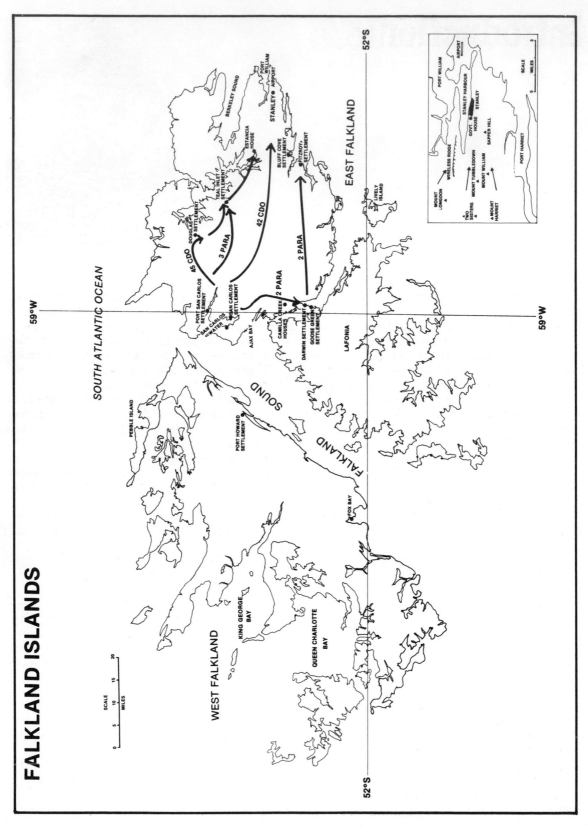

Get them ashore

Commodore Michael Clapp, who master-minded the landings.

The man, who master-minded the amphibious landings in the Falklands, has confessed there was a time when he began to doubt if the British forces could survive the savage Argentinian air strikes.

Commodore Michael Clapp, Commodore Amphibious Warfare, and his staff shouldered the responsibility for getting all the British forces established safely ashore with the vast amount of stores and equipment they needed.

The sister frigates, HMS Ardent and HMS Antelope, were lost on May 21 and 23. The destroyer, HMS Coventry, hit by bombs, and the container ship, Atlantic Conveyor, full of military stores and hit by an Exocet missile, were lost on May 25. Other British ships had been damaged.

"When Coventry was sunk, my heart was firmly in my mouth that we might not be able to hold on in the naval sense," said Commodore Clapp at his headquarters in Plymouth's Stonehouse Barracks.

"The Royal Marines and Paras appeared to be unharmed, but I still needed several more days to unload. I was beginning to worry about getting into a position where the land force could not be built up sufficiently to take Port Stanley and where we had insufficient ships to support them and to protect 5 Infantry Brigade.

"But, thank heavens, it never came to that. If the rate of attrition through air strikes on the first day had continued, I think we would have been very worried indeed," said Commodore Clapp.

"You get into the awful position of wondering how to get troops back off the beach, if you have no assets to get them off. I clearly could not abandon the Royal Marines or the Paras. So we sat there like coconuts, hoping for the best and hitting out at every Argentinian aircraft that came near."

Commodore Clapp, had returned from a visit to Denmark and Germany, where he had been on a reconnaissance for a NATO exercise to find himself plunged into the preparations for the Task Force.

He was in Portsmouth and his immediate actions included giving priority to fitting guns to the logistic landing ships, trying to get a mine counter-measures team organised and trying to get more officers to augment his small staff.

He then flew by helicopter to Plymouth to join Major-General Jeremy Moore and Brigadier Julian Thompson to set up the force.

"At that stage, I did not know what ships I was going to get and they did not know what landing force they would have," said Commodore Clapp. "It seemed clear that 3 Commando Brigade would not be sufficient to push out such large numbers of Argentinians.

"Our staff worked feverishly that first weekend in April, learning about the Falkland Islands from men who had been there. Their knowledge was quite invaluable in helping us set the scene."

He went to the Commander-in-Chief Fleet's headquarters at Northwood on April 4 and it was decided the force should have two battalions of Paras, a squadron of Rapier air-

Commodore Clapp had his headquarters in HMS Fearless, seen here steaming alongside the merchant ship Elk, which was part of his Amphibious Task Group.

defence missiles and two troops of light tanks from the Blues and Royals. A priority was to get more helicopters for troop lifting and logistic support.

Commodore Clapp managed to spend a few hours with his family in Plymouth before flying out to join the assault ship, HMS Fearless, in the Channel on April 6 and take command of the Amphibious Task Group.

"While we were going south, there was tremendous speculation," he said. "There was clearly great political pressure for a show of force and it implied we might have to go straight in.

"That filled us with a certain level of unease because the loading had been done very quickly and we were not sure what was in which ship and in what order.

"We looked at various options like sailing to South Georgia and using the Argentinian force there for a practice assault, and then using the sheltered waters there to re-load our ships before going for the Falklands. That did not meet with much approval at the top because it was thought South Georgia could be cracked easily with other assets."

In the event, the Amphibious Task Group waited off Ascension Island rationalising loads and getting the fighting troops ashore for weapons practice.

The cruise liner, Canberra, and the merchant ships, Europic Ferry, Norland and Elk, were in Commodore Clapp's amphibious group and there were problems in developing procedures for them and practising disembarking the troops they carried in landing craft and helicopters.

Merchant crews were initially under the impression they would not be entering a war zone, but, after Commodore Clapp had sent a series of signals to the Commander-in-Chief, the crews, with few individual exceptions, were only too eager to sail on south.

The amphibious task group sailed from Ascension on May 7 and Commodore Clapp said: "We sailed secretly and I believe we fooled the Russian intelligence ship which was sitting off Ascension."

He revealed that later on the voyage south, the force was picked up by Russian long-range maritime reconnaissance planes, which are believed to operate from Cuba and Luanda.

Norland, normally seen plying the North Sea ferry routes, here disembarks her "new passengers" in San Carlos Water.

The force was overflown as the container ship, Atlantic Conveyor, hastily converted at Devonport to carry Harriers and helicopters, was being refuelled.

Commodore Clapp also revealed that Atlantic Conveyor had a fully-armed Harrier ready on deck to take off and destroy any Argentinian reconnaissance aircraft which attempted to fly near the ships.

On the voyage south from Ascension, Commodore Clapp's staff and that of Brigadier Thompson, who commanded 3 Commando Brigade, worked together to prepare details for the landings. Special Forces were put ashore to gather intelligence.

A number of possible sites were considered and then decided against. Finally, it was agreed San Carlos Water off Falkland Sound was sufficiently land-locked to allow boat work at any time and the hills around it would hamper air attacks and make it easier to defend against a counter-attack.

Commodore Clapp said it was the logical choice and, like other possible sites, was carefully reconnoitred by Special Boat Section men trained to make evaluations for amphibious landings. Arguments against the choice of San Carlos Water included the fact that it could be mined, was deep enough for Argentinian submarines to operate and was

rather too far from Port Stanley.

"As we got closer, we were more and more worried about the air threat," said Commodore Clapp. "Rear-Admiral Woodward had not been able to draw out the Argentinian air force. We were aware of Exocet and we did not like it."

"I knew we would be under fairly heavy air attack when we went in. I saw the air threat as the major problem, but it was not the only one. There were many places where Argentinian patrol craft or midget submarines, which we knew they have, could lie up and then attack," he said.

"We were deeply concerned that we had all our eggs in one basket with three battalions of troops in Canberra, and, amazingly, on May 19 Fearless and Intrepid docked down in flat calm seas in the Roaring Forties for a Commando and a Parachute battalion to be taken off the liner."

The amphibious force made its approach in a very tight formation on May 20.

"We were in glorious thick weather," said Commodore Clapp. "It was just what we wanted. It was really marvellous. I remember saying to Brigadier Thompson that someone must be on our side.

"It was very frightening going in because we knew we were going in to create a honeypot. There was the distinct feeling of generations of naval officers sitting on one's shoulder saying 'don't worry, we have all been through this'. Initially, my main worry was stumbling over an Argentinian submarine."

Special Boat Section men were already ashore, but the mist, which masked the approach of the amphibious force, had reduced their field of vision to about 200 yards near the shore and less than that on the hills.

"We had reports of enemy on Fanning

Head so we found out where they were by some rather crafty means and put in a patrol to get them out," said Commodore Clapp.

In the early hours of May 21, the first troops were going ashore and the plan was to take and hold the high ground before daylight and to get the gun batteries and Rapier missiles ashore before the inevitable air attacks began.

Most of the troops were ashore by dawn. Two Puccaras were the first Argentinian planes on the scene and then the air strikes really began in earnest. About a week was needed to unload all the stores and equipment for the break-out towards Port Stanley.

Commodore Clapp, who had formerly commanded a Buccaneer squadron, knew only too well that the hills around San Carlos Water would hamper the incoming enemy planes.

"It was not luck that the Argentinian pilots attacked the warships and not the landing ships," he said.

"We had lots of time to think about it and the whole approach to the landings had been a threat reduction exercise."

The warships were placed so that the Argentinians had to fly close to them to get at the amphibious ships. Guns of every calibre were pressed into service and an enormous amount of tracer was fired to make the Argentinian pilots twist and turn and to make it impossible for them to aim accurately.

Commodore Clapp had 19 ships on D-Day and he could not get them all in San Carlos Water. He believed it was essential to achieve surprise and to land all the troops and their most vital equipment on the first day.

"If I tried to do it in penny numbers, I was liable to failure," he said. "That is why I took in Canberra. Since she was mainly a troop carrier, she had actually done her job by daylight. It was a calculated risk to take her in for one day to offload."

After the first day, Commodore Clapp drew the escorts into San Carlos Water to continue

Major units of the landing force left to right RFA Stromness, HMS Fearless, Canberra & Atlantic Conveyor seen from HMS Intrepid.

Sunrise at San Carlos . . . A machine-gun team from 40 Cdo. on board Canberra as she slips into San Carlos water on D-Day.

A calculated risk . . . Commodore Clapp decided to take Canberra right into the action on D-Day. Seen here in San Carlos water with HMS Andromeda.

No turning back. The first troops head for the beaches. Would their landing be opposed?

their vital job of providing air defence.Crews of landing craft, Mexeflotes and helicopters worked long hours ferrying stores ashore.

The two Guards battalions and the Gurkhas in 5 Infantry Brigade finally arrived and went ashore but the amphibious assault proper was completed by May 26.

The Welsh Guards and a Field Ambulance unit had to be sent forward by logistic landing ship because it was not possible to fly or march them forward.

Commodore Clapp said he had been surprised when the Welsh Guards and the Field Ambulance failed to disembark from Sir Galahad at Fitzroy before the ship was attacked with such tragic loss of life.

"Tragedy struck, perhaps, because we were all running a little fast," he said. "Communications were always difficult and my staff and I were more used to dealing with Royal Marines, who are trained to get off a ship as quickly as possible, than with soldiers, inexperienced in amphibious operations."

He believed the British forces had done extremely well and the Harriers had survived far better than expected. When the surrender came on June 14, naval gun ammunition was running low because of the intense shore bombardments.

He talked of the immense problems of eva-

The beach-head is established. Men and machinery move ashore.

"So we sat there like coconuts, hoping for the best and hitting out at every Argentinian aircraft that came near" —
Commodore Clapp.

Offloading men and machinery into small craft is a long and slow process. The arrival of Argentinian Mirage fighters only made matters worse. This aircraft overflying RFA Sir Bedivere was shot down seconds later as it passed over other task force ships.

cuating large numbers of casualties and of dealing with the many prisoners of war. He had only praise for the merchant ships and for the way two extra squadrons of helicopters were "conjured up somehow from somewhere".

Commodore Clapp said Fearless and Intrepid, which had once faced the axe, proved their worth every day. The brunt of the war had fallen on the logistic landing ships, which were only lightly armed.

"I had to take risks with the logistic landing ships and I explained to them the size of the risk I was asking them to take," he said. "Fitzroy was the only time it went bad for me."

He added: "I would like to see a craft between an open landing craft and the old tank landing craft. I needed something smaller than a logistic landing ship but capable of carrying one or two days supplies of food and ammunition."

What did he feel after the surrender? "I was just glad it was all over," he said. "I did not particularly enjoy it. I am not sure I shall ever enjoy looking back on it."

Commodore Clapp added: "I was quite overwhelmed at times by the spirit and superb determination of the sailors and the officers.

"For three weeks we sat at anchor in a great tin ship. You wondered how they could miss during air attacks. If a bomb had fallen on a ship, a lot of people would have been killed or maimed. The men were very courageous."

Sink the Belgrano

Commander Christopher Wreford-Brown, RN, captain of the nuclear powered submarine HMS Conqueror.

The captain of the nuclear-powered submarine, HMS Conqueror, was watching through the periscope as two of his torpedoes hit the Argentinian cruiser, General Belgrano, on May 2.

Commander Christopher Wreford-Brown recalled: "I saw one hit amidships. I saw a fireball. I saw a cloud of dirty smoke as the second torpedo hit."

Those two Mark 8 diesel-driven torpedoes spelt the end for the elderly cruiser, which as USS Phoenix had survived the Japanese attack on Pearl Harbour in World War II.

Conqueror had fired a salvo of three torpedoes, but all three had not been expected to hit the target.

Commander Wreford-Brown wasted no time after seeing his attack had been successful. He ordered that his boat should dive deep and put some distance between her and the counter-attack he expected from General Belgrano's two escorting destroyers.

He had been in command for three weeks when Conqueror was ordered to sail south from Faslane early in April, after completing a maintenance period and storing for war.

Secrecy always surrounds the depth and speed of submarines, but Commander Wreford-Brown said Conqueror had been "deep" and making over 20 knots for the long voyage to the South Atlantic.

"On the way south, we were updated with likely requirements, the rules of engagement and the likely threat," he said. "We headed first for the vicinity of South Georgia to set up an anti-ship and anti-submarine patrol in defence of the force sent to re-take South Georgia.

The 285ft-long submarine moves deep and silent on patrol. Her electronic ears can pick up ships at substantial ranges, depending on weather conditions, and submarines at shorter ranges.

Her main sonar is a passive listening device on her bows. In addition, her periscope enables her to search visually for ships and planes and she has sensitive equipment for detecting other ships' radars.

"We can either be deep listening on sonar or at periscope depth using the other two methods," said Commander Wreford-Brown. "Off South Georgia, we were looking for ships or submarines trying to reinforce the Argentinians ashore."

Conqueror remained in the area until South Georgia was re-occupied by British troops and then moved west to the waters around the Falkland Islands. Her patrol took her around the outer limits of the Total Exclusion Zone declared by the Government.

"We were tasked to look for and find the General Belgrano group," said Commander Wreford-Brown. "It was reported to consist of the cruiser and escorts. We located her on our passive sonar and sighted her visually early on the afternoon of May 1.

"We took up a position astern and followed the General Belgrano for over 30 hours. We reported that we were in contact with her. We remained several miles astern and deep below her. We had instructions to attack if she went inside the Total Exclusion Zone.

"I think the ship's company in Conqueror felt we were waiting for things to develop. I felt it was bound to escalate."

Commander Wreford-Brown said that on May 2 he received a signal from the Commander-in-Chief Fleet's headquarters at Northwood which made a change in the rules of engagement and allowed him to attack the Argentinian cruiser outside the TEZ.

"She was 20 to 30 miles outside the TEZ and, in everyone's eyes, posed a threat to the Task Group," said Commander Wreford-Brown.

"The scenario changed from one of following to one of going in for an attack. I was several miles astern at that time. I worked myself into an attacking position on her port beam by using my speed.

"I fired a salvo of three Mark 8 torpedoes from about 1,400 yards. They were fired at short intervals. I was at periscope depth doing a visual attack.

"We knew the range and we had timed how long it would take the torpedoes to run. I looked through the periscope and saw two of the torpedoes hit.

"My immediate reaction was to clear my position from where I had fired. We went deep and used our speed to move away. At the time, I felt glad I had conducted a successful attack and I was then concentrating on avoiding what I presumed would be a counter-attack by her escorts, two ex-US Navy Sumner-class destroyers, which carried some form of depth charges."

Commander Wreford-Brown said his ship's company heard the explosions as the torpedoes struck home and cheers went up in the submarine.

"We had successfully got into the position to carry out our attack, which is what we had been sent to do," said Commander Wreford-Brown.

"Afterwards I had a certain amount of

HMS Conqueror returns to her base on the Clyde proudly flying the first "Jolly Roger" seen since World War II.

regret about the loss of life. I did not know the numbers involved, but one presumed it was considerable.

"We had countered the threat the General Belgrano offered to our Task Group and the loss of life they could have caused us.

"Now I feel we did just what we were invited to do and I would have no hesitation in doing it again. It is a fact of life that if you want to go to war, you must expect losses.

"They would not have been there if they had not accepted the risks. The escorting destroyers took a certain amount of interest in the area in which they presumed we were for a short time. We moved several miles away to report what had happened to Northwood via satellite."

Commander Wreford-Brown said he was keen to get away from the vicinity of the attack because he believed the Argentinians would mount a search for his submarine with maritime patrol aircraft.

Conqueror stayed in the South Atlantic until after the Argentinian surrender. She patrolled looking for Argentinian ships or submarines posing a threat to British forces.

During the campaign, one of her communications wires became wrapped around her propellor. It caused the screw to vibrate at speed and seriously increased the chances of her being detected by enemy ships or submarines.

"We surfaced at night and my best diver, Petty Officer Graham Libby, volunteered to dive in marginal weather to clear the wire from the propellor," said Commander Wreford-Brown. "He was diving in the dark in a reasonably rough sea.

"He spent 20 minutes struggling to get the wire off. Before he went out, I had to warn him that, if there was an air attack, I would have to dive and this would have given him very little time to get back on board.

"I think he was outstandingly brave. It is just the sort of thing I would expect from him."

Petty Officer Libby, 23, was awarded the DSM for this exploit.

Conqueror turned for home in mid-June and surfaced near the Equator to receive a mail-drop from the RAF.

That mail drop was much appreciated by the submariners and they were delighted when their captain gave permission for them to leap over the side for a swim in a sea at a tropical 87 degrees Fahrenheit.

The "Jolly Roger", traditional sign of a successful patrol, was flying proudly from Conqueror's bridge when she arrived back at Faslane.

Her attack on General Belgrano, which posed such a threat with its 15 six-inch guns and eight five-inch guns, was the first torpedo attack by a submarine since World War II.

Commander Wreford-Brown, who was awarded the DSO in the Falklands Honours List, said the medal was a reflection of the performance of the whole of his ship's company throughout the patrol.

"I think the patrol moulded the team together," he said. "There is nothing special about us. I believe any other British submarine could have been equally successful. It just happened to be us at the time. It has made us unique, rather than special. That is the subtle difference as a team."

Commander Wreford-Brown said his ship's company had an average age of early 20's. All had learned a lot about themselves and each other during the campaign.

"It was a privilege to lead such a team down there," he said. "I would do it all again. We all believe what we were doing was right and necessary. It is what we have trained for and it is something any submarine in the flotilla was capable of doing at very short notice."

War in the air

The major contribution to the air war in the South Atlantic came from the Royal Naval Air Station Yeovilton, which sent a total of about 120 Sea Harriers and helicopters and some 1,400 officers and men.

Nine squadrons, three of them formed especially for the campaign, left Yeovilton to do battle and twelve men from the station gave their lives in the bitter fighting.

Sea Harrier pilots, out-numbered 20-1 by the Argentinian Air Force at the beginning, flew sorties night and day to protect the fleet and to strike at shore targets. Their pilots became used to sitting strapped in their cockpits on the decks of HMS Hermes and HMS Invincible for long hours, ready to scramble at a few minutes notice.

By the end of the campaign, 31 "kills" were attributed to Sea Harriers. 24 Argentinian aircraft were shot down with air-launched missiles; the rest were destroyed by fire from the twin 30 mm cannon carried in the Sea Harriers.

Yeovilton's Sea Harriers in the campaign came from 899, 800 and 801 Squadrons and from the now disbanded 809 Squadron.

Lynx helicopters from 815 Squadron served in the majority of Task Force ships and the Sea King Mk 4's from 846 Squadron had a vital role throughout the campaign.

Wessex Mk 5's from Yeovilton were in 845 Squadron and in 847 and 848 Squadrons, which have since disbanded. Like the Sea Kings, they were involved in a great deal of cross-decking on the voyage south. Some were involved in operations with Special Forces and, once the British landing had been made, they flew tirelessly in support of ground operations.

Six Yeovilton Sea Harriers were lost, two in a tragic mid-air collision while flying from HMS Invincible in very poor visibility. One was lost in heavy weather, another hit the sea while night flying. Lt. Nick Taylor's plane was shot down at Goose Green and a surface-to-air missile claimed a sixth.

Lt.Cdr. Robin Kent, who was Mentioned in Despatches, flew as senior pilot with 801 Squadron in Invincible. On May 1 his squadron flew as air defence for the Sea Harriers from Hermes making strikes at Port Stanley airfield and Goose Green.

"I was in the first engagement that morning," said Lt.Cdr. Kent. "I had missiles launched against me from Mirage III's, but they missed. It was a high-speed intercept. They turned and ran and we could not catch them. I saw a missile go about 30 to 40 yards away, above me and to the right. The missiles had been fired from about 4½ miles.

"I had no time to worry. I was concentrating on getting on to him. But the missiles brought a lot of reality to the situation."

Lt.Cdr. Kent said the British pilots' problem was picking up enemy aircraft in time to get into position to intercept them. Hermes and Invincible were operating some 200 miles from the islands and it gave the Sea Harriers only a short period on task.

He recalled a "fair amount of flak" a few days later when he made a bombing and photo reconnaissance run over Port Stanley

Flagship of the force—HMS Hermes. Her decks crowded with Wessex and Sea King helicopters.

airfield at 10,000ft. After that, the minimum height for attacks on the airfield became 20,000ft.

Combat air patrols around the Falklands were maintained by the Sea Harriers, with a pair being launched every 20 minutes. The two aircraft kept on deck at 5 minutes notice day and night were a great drain on manpower. The superb servicability record of the aircraft was a tribute to the dedicated work of the maintenance crews.

Lt.Cdr. Kent was on combat air patrol when HMS Coventry was hit on May 25. "I saw her turn over," he said. "I was sent out to look for possible contacts and when I returned, she had virtually gone under. You could just see the hull shape level with the water. It was pretty unpleasant. I don't like to see mighty ships like that going down."

He recalled the alert for possible Exocet attack when he returned to Invincible. The same thing happened again on May 30.

"It was interesting trying to get back on board when the fleet was under the threat of missile attack," said Lt.Cdr. Kent. "You became a low priority and there was the inevitability of running out of fuel.

"They always had to point the ship at the threat and on both occasions I had to land out of wind across the deck. The tables are turned very quickly. They have to worry about the ship. Getting you back on board is incidental. You have five minutes to play with or you have to jump out. If your motor stops, you don't glide in, you go down."

He described the period as "very intensive flying" but he said none of the pilots was unduly worried by the risks. "That is the flying game," he said. "We live with the risks on a regular basis.

"The aircraft were outstanding. The servicability was such that only about one per cent of all the sorties tasked were lost. There is nothing in the world to touch the aircraft. We

Sunk three times according to the Argentinian propaganda machine, HMS Invincible at speed on patrol off the Falklands.

Two of "The Few". A Naval and RAF Harrier over-fly HMS Broadsword. British pilots faced odds of 20-to 1 at the beginning of the campaign.

have a good weapons system coupled with the Sidewinder missile. It is a very potent combination.

"The missiles proved to be far more effective than we had believed and certainly more than the Argentinians believed," said Lt.Cdr. Kent.

Looking back on the campaign he said: "The effectiveness of our training is the key for me. We were not asked to do anything we had not trained for. Because of that, we had sufficient confidence to achieve the aim. On the way down, the odds were 20 to 1. They had 240 combat aircraft. We had 20. One obviously went into it with a little reticence because of the odds. But I found that if you stuck to your training, you ended up on top."

Lt. Nigel North, training officer with 846 Squadron, was awarded the Distinguished Service Cross for his exceptional qualities of professionalism, courage and leadership. The citation said he made an outstanding contribution to the success of 26 operational night sorties carried out by his squadron between May 1 and 19.

The sorties were to insert, re-supply and extract reconnaissance patrols throughout East and West Falkland in the build-up to the British landing. The squadron played a leading part in the Pebble Island attack.

It was Lt. North's responsiblity to work up selected crews at short notice in the use of new tactics, techniques and equipment. He led the formation in the first mission and flew 28 of these difficult sorties, including the Pebble Island operation.

He recalled that on the night of the Pebble Island raid, in which Special Forces destroyed Argentinian planes and equipment, there were 50 knots of wind across the deck of HMS Hermes.

"The ship had to steam into the wind to get

All quiet on HMS Hermes flight deck. Fog and low cloud kept the Argentinian Air Force away as well as grounding our own aircraft on a few occasions.

where she had to be," said Lt. North. "It made life for the maintainers getting the aircraft ready for night flying very difficult and hazardous. They did a magnificent job.

"Once we got airborne, the weather was not too bad. The operation was very demanding because it was very important. There were a lot of men involved. It had to go right otherwise we would have lost a lot of guys."

Lt. North led the aircraft going in. The Special Forces were landed and the helicopters returned later to take them off. "We could see the fires of hell burning from about 15 miles away," said Lt. North. "It had gone quite well for them. There were a couple of men slightly injured. They were working against the odds and it was to their tremendous credit they achieved what thcy did."

Sea Kings from 846 Squadron flew on the decoy raid in the Goose Green area the night before the British landing. It was very successful, with a handful of Special Forces conning the Argentinians into believing it was, perhaps, a battalion-sized operation.

Night operations demanded a great deal of the pilots. The featureless islands were a great test of navigation, with hills looking similar and few rivers and streams.

After the landing at San Carlos, 846 Squadron went ashore to begin resupplying the bridgehead before the move east to Port Stanley. The hectic programme of moving guns, ammunition and stores was combined with operations with Special Forces. Lt. North's aircraft was hit by a round from a machine-gun as he attempted to pick up a casualty from Darwin.

The squadron's commanding officer, Lt.Cdr. Simon Thornewill, who was awarded the DSC., had a very narrow escape on June 13 in the Mount Kent area, when his Sea King was attacked by four Skyhawks. With the help of his aircrewman, CPO Malcolm Tupper, who was awarded the DSM, he was able to execute a series of manoeuvres and succeeded in evading the fighters. But a 30 mm cannon shell went through the main spar of his helicopter's rotor.

Lt. North, who picked up about 20 survivors when HMS Coventry was sunk, said: "The flying was very demanding and very satisfying for us. We had to develop new techniques in a big hurry and they proved successful. We did not lose any aircraft or people through enemy action, although we had some losses from accidents, which is not unusual in wartime when the pressure is on."

Lt.Cdr. Jack Lomas went south in the RFA Resource as flight commander with two Wessex 5's from 845 Squadron. He assumed command of aircraft from the squadron when they arrived in the Falklands, ending up with seven aircraft and a team of about 140 men.

The citation for his DSC refers to his "determined and gallant leadership in the air, often in the face of air attack and enemy ground fire". The achievement of his detachment was described as "noteworthy" and his contribution to the support of the ground forces as "substantial".

Two of 845 Squadron's Wessex 5's in the RFA Tidespring crashed on the Fortuna Glacier in South Georgia while on operations with Special Forces. Their pilots flew in appalling weather to insert men from the SAS, who then endured a night in such violent weather they had to be withdrawn next day.

The two Wessex from Tidespring and a Wessex from HMS Antrim went in to recover them. Lt. Mike Tidd's Wessex from 845 Squadron crashed in a white-out. The aircrew and troops were picked up by the remaining two helicopters.

Shortly after, the second Wessex from 845 Squadron crashed in the appalling weather. Antrim's helicopter flew her passengers to the ship and returned to recover the party from the second crashed aircraft. Everyone from the operation was recovered safely.

The men from 845 flight in Tidespring found themselves with no aircraft and became guards for the Argentinian prisoners from South Georgia for the voyage to Ascension Island where they were re-equipped with two more Wessex.

Lt.Cdr. Lomas was involved in the rescue operation when HMS Sheffield was hit by an Exocet missile on May 4. "When she was hit, we could see the smoke from 20 miles away. Our main job was carrying pumps and medical teams from Hermes and other ships to Sheffield and to Arrow and Yarmouth, which were assisting her," he said.

"I went back a second time to take people off the back of Arrow. Sheffield was a horrific sight. We knew that if another Exocet attack came and Resource was hit, we would not survive because she was full of ammunition."

He said the next two weeks were spent in

flying ammunition from Resource to frigates involved in naval gunfire support operations on shore targets. His flight arrived in San Carlos on May 23 and disembarked next day to move ashore. Other 845 aircraft were to join him later.

The Royal Navy flyers found themselves living rough ashore as they continued the important tasks of off-loading ships and moving supplies forward. During the frequent air attacks, the pilots sought cover in the folds of ground around San Carlos.

Lt.Cdr. Lomas said: "The danger was not so much from enemy aircraft, but from our own ships. The amount of lead and missiles going up from them had to come down. We had one aircraft with a bullet hole through the co-pilot's windscreen. Luckily, he was not in his seat at the time.

"We modified our hiding positions not only to hide from enemy aircraft, but to keep out of line of our own ships," he said.

When the Royal Marines and Paras began the move towards Port Stanley, Lt.Cdr. Lomas took his aircraft over to Port San Carlos. "Alan Miller, the settlement manager, was a super guy. He welcomed us with open arms. Basically, we took over his house and the aircrew lived in his conference room.

"Our maintainers put up tents in his garden. We used his cow byre as a galley and the garage as an operations centre. We had cover and somewhere to cook. We had 'won' some of the kit we needed to live. But the only cooking utensil we had at that stage was a 2-inch rocket projectile container about the size of a gash bin. It was used at all times for pot mess," said Lt.Cdr. Lomas.

845 Squadron's aircraft remained at Port San Carlos with forward operating bases at Teal and Fitzroy. Re-supply and casualty evacuation continued until the surrender and there were many hectic days of flying after the white flag went up over Port Stanley.

Lt.Cdr. David Baston commanded 848 Squadron, which was formed with Wessex 5's especially for the crisis and has since disbanded. Six of his aircraft went south in

Airborne freight service—"old faithful" Wessex played a vital part throughout the operation. Seen here off-loading ammunition as the advance continues.

Royal Fleet Auxiliaries and he embarked with the remaining six in the ill-fated Atlantic Conveyor from Devonport.

He was manning a machine gun on the bridge when the container ship was hit by an Exocet missile on May 25. She had been steaming towards the Falklands ready to unload the following day. His six Wessex and the three Chinooks and a Lynx on board were all lost.

Lt.Cdr. Baston and many other survivors were picked up from their liferafts by the frigate, HMS Alacrity, which had made a vain attempt to fight the fire in the blazing Atlantic Conveyor. He returned to Ascension Island in British Tay and was flown home by the RAF.

"Our disappointment was to have worked so hard during the time at sea, to have got so far and not been able to get in on the final act," said Lt.Cdr. Baston.

Lt.Cdr. Mike Crabtree, a flight commander in 845 Squadron, flew his Wessex 5 on operations with Special Forces in the San Carlos area the night before the British landing. On D-Day his aircraft was tasked to evacuate casualties. He saw the explosion as HMS Ardent was hit and flew to assist.

"The ship was listing and on fire from just forward of the hangar all the way back," he said. "The flight deck had gone completely and smoke was pouring out all over it. There were small explosions and some people in the water."

Surgeon Commander Rick Jolly, who ran the hospital at Ajax Bay, was in Lt.Cdr. Crabtree's helicopter and he did not hesitate when a sailor in the water was unable to grasp the strop lowered to him from the aircraft.

The commando-trained naval doctor, who was wearing only combat clothing, went down in the strop, grasped the survivor in his arms and brought him safely back up to the helicopter.

Lt.Cdr. Crabtree said: "I remember that first day most vividly. I was nervous, but it was a nervous excitement. There was lots of adrenalin. I rather enjoyed it when it was going on. But we never got complacent.

"The most moving thing was when we helped with the Galahad rescue. When we got to Fitzroy, most of the men had been brought ashore and it was a case of taking casualties from Fitzroy to the Ajax Bay hospital.

"What almost brought tears to my eyes

were the Chinese crewmen standing around looking utterly bewildered. There was sheer disbelief on their faces. They looked completely and utterly down and out. A lot were quite elderly. They looked as if they could not hurt a fly."

Lt.Cdr. Crabtree said: "I remember the elation of my first look at Port Stanley. I remember thinking 'that is what we have come for'. It was marvellous. After that it was an anticlimax. But we still had a lot of work to do and a tremendous amount of flying in front of us."

Sub.Lt. Paul Heathcote, 21, flew as co-pilot with Lt.Cdr. Crabtree and was one of the youngest pilots from Yeovilton in the South Atlantic. He had been awarded his wings almost one year to the day before the British went ashore at San Carlos.

He had joined a front-line squadron only four months before the conflict. "It was good," he said. "A lot of people said it was horrible. But I did not find it like that. It was interesting flying and you learned a lot in a short time.

"It was like a big game. You treat it like a big game until you get hit and then it tends to sour a bit."

Petty Officers Steve Boden and Jim Tims, both aircraft mechanics with 848 Squadron in the Falklands, were among the many men, who used small arms against attacking Argentinian jets. They remained on board the Norland for several days after she arrived in San Carlos.

"We had had a couple of raids and we were sort of getting used to it," said PO Tims. "A Mirage came over the top and turned alongside us. It was very low and belly on to us. We thought it might cartwheel. We fired at it with self-loading rifles and it went away trailing smoke. I had fired 17 rounds. We could see them striking.

"We were feeling mad. We were sort of saying 'who the hell do you think you are'."

PO Boden said: "The Mirage was only about 100 metres away. It was banked right over and gave us a good target. There were about 20 of us shooting at it with rifles. You could see the rounds hitting the plane. We saw flashes on the wings and smoke started pouring from the engine. We met Royal Marines later, who told us the pilot had ejected and been killed.

"I had wondered if I could fire to kill when

Round the clock flying inevitably brought problems. This Sea King ditched and eventually sank after the crew had been rescued. Thanks to tireless work by maintainers, mechanical failures were few.

it came to the crunch," said PO Boden. "But at the time, nothing passes through your mind. It was very exciting. Afterwards, we were all shaking. We felt unprotected on deck, but it gave us a chance to have a go back. It made us feel a lot better."

Chief Petty Officer David Thompson, of 845 Squadron, talked of the difficulties the ground crews experienced in working on aircraft ashore with few facilities. A job that normally took one hour would take three or four times as long because of the cold.

"I'm glad I was there," he said. "It was nice to be part of a team which was taking part in some real work for a change, as opposed to N years of exercises. It was good to see everything working as it should and did.

"The thing that struck me most of all was the quality of the young men with us. They never baulked or hesitated once. For all the criticism the young take today, it showed down in the Falklands that they would jump to it when told because they knew there was a good reason behind it. They were very good. I can't praise them enough."

Air to air refuelling

The RAF were kept busy, too. The massive distances involved meant RAF pilots had to re-learn old skills on aircraft not normally refuelled in the air.

A Hercules tanker refuelling a Hercules transport during the long flight from Ascension to Port Stanley. Even after hostilities ceased the 'air bridge' to and from Stanley could only be maintained—at great cost—by refuelling aircraft in mid air, on their 13 hour journey.

A Hercules refuelling from a Vulcan bomber—converted to a tanker during the conflict.

A Victor tanker refuelling a Nimrod submarine hunter on a long sortie from Ascension Island.

Arrow in action

HMS Arrow's 4.5-inch gun boomed. Smoke plumed away from the menacing barrel. Several miles away there was the flash of an explosion on Port Stanley airfield.

It was May 1 and the Type 21 frigate had fired the first British shell at the Falkland Islands. Soon she was to find herself under attack.

Arrow had been on a big exercise in the Mediterranean when she was ordered to sail south for the Falklands. One of her main tasks, apart from escorting the carriers Hermes and Invincible, was to bombard shore targets in support of military operations.

May 1 saw her a few miles off Port Stanley in company with her sister-ship, Alacrity, and the County-class destroyer, Glamorgan.

"Arrow was the first ship to fire at the Falklands," said Lt. Andrew Jackman, 23. "We had fired our allocated rounds and we were withdrawing back out to sea when we saw an Argentinian aircraft shot down by Argentinian guns over Port Stanley.

"We learned later that it was a Mirage. We could see tracer and other anti-aircraft fire hitting the plane and it plummeted like a white ball into the sea.

"As we continued withdrawing, three Mirages attacked our group of ships. They flew across Glamorgan firing their guns. We replied with our 20mm Oerlikon.

"One of the planes hit our superstructure around the funnel with nine cannon shells. There was no serious damage to the ship, but an able seaman was hit by shrapnel in the chest," said Lt. Jackman.

AB Ian Britnell, the first British casualty of the war, was treated aboard Arrow before being airlifted to Hermes.

"I went to speak to him in the sick bay," recalled Lt. Jackman. "He was conscious and able to speak, but it hurt him if he tried to laugh."

That air attack did nothing to impair Arrow's fighting capability, but it had a dramatic effect on her ship's company.

"The effect of the attack was quite surprising," said Lt. Jackman. "Everyone suddenly realised it was for real. I don't think people realised we would be fighting down there. I think everyone thought the Argentinians would cry off.

"Everyone was working together before the attack, but it seemed even better after the attack. Our morale certainly went up. Arrow was battle-hardened."

Leading Radio Operator Jim Cunningham, 27, echoed that sentiment.

"That first day when AB Britnell was injured brought reality home to us," he said. "We were not messing around. It was serious then. I think in the beginning everyone was saying it was not going to happen.

"We had fired shells, but we had fired on exercises. We did not expect them to shoot back at us. I was on the bridge when we were hit. I saw the aircraft coming across.

"You could see the cannon shells bouncing off the water and getting closer to the ship. I took a flying leap to the other side of the bridge out of the way."

CPO Neil Van Landewyck, 37, said: "That attack woke us up and got the message home to us that it was a real shooting match rather than a flexing of muscles."

Arrow went back in close to land for another bombardment that night and after that her bombardments and that of other Task Force ships were at night wherever possible because of the threat of air attacks during daylight.

Three days later, on May 4, the world was shocked to hear that the Type 42 destroyer, HMS Sheffield, had been hit by an Exocet missile while on radar picket duty with the battle-group.

Arrow, only a few miles from the stricken warship, was ordered to speed to her rescue as flames began to engulf Sheffield.

For several hours, Arrow remained secured alongside Sheffield providing fire pumps, hoses, breathing apparatus and other equip-ment for what was to be a losing battle against the flames.

Fortunately conditions were calm with a slight swell and little wind. Men in Arrow played hoses on to Sheffield and Arrow's fire main was plugged into Sheffield because the destroyer had lost all power—and thus her firemain.

Food, drink and sweets were passed to Sheffield's men during those long hours of fire-fighting. Two badly burned men were taken aboard the frigate for treatment until they could be airlifted to Hermes.

Leading Cook Chris Jones, 33, had pre-viously served in Sheffield and he was horrified when he saw his old ship.

"Seeing Sheffield shocked and frightened me," he said. "When I looked at the hole made by the missile, I knew the galley had been seriously damaged.

"I had left Sheffield in 1979, but the chefs'

First battle damage of the campaign. HMS Arrow's funnel tells its own story after an air attack.

HMS Arrow (left) leads the desperate fight to save HMS Sheffield, crippled by an Exocet attack.

branch is close-knit and I knew all the chefs on board her. I was heartbroken to see the ship in that state."

Leading Radio Operator Cunningham said he recalled dirty, dazed men from Sheffield coming aboard Arrow with their clothing soaking wet when the destroyer was eventually abandoned.

"You thought, I've seen this in the movies. You thought it's bloody true. Some of them did not know where they were or what they were doing. You thought what could happen so easily to you," said Leading Radio Operator Cunningham.

"One thing I remember was a body wrapped in a blanket on Sheffield's fo'c'sle. I can still see it. It is one thing I will always remember," he said.

CPO Van Landewyck said: "It was pretty horrific. I had never seen a ship burning like that. I helped a first aid party carry a bad burns case which they transfered to us.

"When you see that kind of thing, someone with their skin all blackened and still conscious, you get to thinking it could have been me. It made you realise the kind of injuries that were going to be sustained.

"At the time you were too busy to think about it. But, looking back, it was pretty frightening."

CPO Van Landewyck added: "The thing that got me was thinking about the 20 bodies going down with the ship."

Arrow took on board 224 men from Sheffield—her own ship's company was about 180—and all the survivors were given dry clothing, a hot meal and a bunk or a mattress for the night.

"What were the survivors like? What you would expect people to be like after their home had been wrecked and they had lost friends and everything they had," said Lt. Jackman.

"They were very quiet. A lot tried to be cheerful, chatting and laughing. But you could see that deep down it was over for them and they realised it."

Arrow sustained some structural damage while alongside Sheffield when the swell thrust the two hulls together.

Between May 4 and May 21, which was D-Day for the British landings in the Falklands, Arrow was involved in a number of special operations and in operations to provide gunfire support for military oper-

ations ashore. She fired over 1,000 rounds in this important role.

There was disbelief at first aboard Arrow when it was learned that her sister-ship, Ardent, had been sunk on May 21. After a second sister-ship, Antelope, was hit on May 23, Arrow was herself ordered into "bomb alley".

Lt. Jackman was on Arrow's bridge as the frigate steamed towards the Falklands and, from a range of about 40 miles, he saw a brilliant flash way ahead over the horizon. He later learned that it was the massive explosion which spelt the end for Antelope.

"With Ardent and Antelope having been hit, people were a bit dubious about what it would be like in bomb alley," said Lt. Jackman.

"We arrived early on May 24 and we were attacked twice that first day. Bombs dropped by one plane missed our stern by about 20 yards, if that. We fired everything we had at the attacking aircraft.

"Small arms and even Very pistols were used. Anything that could fire was fired. We fired into the air to try to put the Argentinian pilots off and it worked.

"The first attack was from two Skyhawks. I was on the bridge. They came in low and fast and then they were gone. We were credited with hitting two aircraft that day," said Lt. Jackman.

Arrow remained in bomb alley for 14 days, with her ship's company at action stations every day from before dawn to well after dusk. At night, she slipped out to bombard shore targets or to escort ships moving in and out of Falkland Sound.

Her shells, fired with devastating accuracy, supported 2 Para's attack on Goose Green and Darwin. She finally left bomb alley on June 7 and went back out to join the carrier group. She continued bombardments until the surrender on June 14.

Arrow sailed back into Devonport on July 7 and the RAF's crack Red Arrows roared overhead in tribute to their namesake.

Lt. Jackman said: "I would not have missed the experience. I was glad I was down there. The men were fantastic. Our training was right. The ship came back home closer knit, still as a family."

Lt. Cdr. Graham Churton, the operations officer, praised the ship's company for their work during the long weeks in the South Atlantic.

The Red Arrows fly past in tribute to their own adopted warship on its return from the South Atlantic.

He described bomb alley as a return to Second World War tactics because radars were badly affected by the close proximity of the land.

"We had to resort to Second World War tactics with about 15 people on the upper deck firing anything that would fire," he said. "We had very intensive look-outs. It was back to the mark one eyeball because of land return from the radar and low-flying aircraft."

Lt.Cdr. Churton added: "I was dealing in the operations room with lads many of whom were only 18 and we sank or swam on their expertise.

"One thing that came out of it was that no-one was under-trained. They put in God-awful hours, particularly in bomb alley. On one occasion the ship was at action stations for 23½ hours without a break.

"They were still able to turn round at the end of a day like that and show they were still doing their job bloody well."

Leading Cook Jones recalled: "Bomb alley was an experience and a half. We went in when Antelope was lost and we were still there 14 days later. It was bloody frightening. I'm no hero. I lay down on the floor of the galley or the dining room lots of times during air raids."

He went on: "I will never forget it. I often wondered whether I would come back home. When you see two ships from the 21 Club (a nickname for the 4th Frigate Squadron) are lost and you know people in them, you begin to wonder.

"I am not a religious man, but I prayed every single night I was down there. And I think 95 per cent of the rest of the ship's company prayed as well."

Helicopter heroes

The light helicopters of 3rd Commando Brigade Air Squadron were in the thick of the action in the battle for the Falklands. Tragically two aircraft were shot down with the loss of three lives on D-Day at San Carlos.

A third helicopter from the squadron, was hit by enemy fire on that first day of the British Landings, but managed to limp back to its parent ship.

Throughout the campaign the squadron's Gazelles and Scouts flew long hours, often at night and in appalling weather. They evacuated hundreds of battle casualties, both British and Argentinian, frequently under fire and ferried ammunition and equipment forward to the fighting troops on the ground.

Tragedy struck the squadron on the day 2 Para fought to victory against great odds at Goose Green. A Scout piloted by Lt. Richard Nunn was shot down by an Argentinian Pucara aircraft.

Lt. Nunn was killed and his aircrewman, Sgt. Bill Belcher, lost a leg. Lt. Nunn was posthumously awarded the Distinguished Flying Cross.

The squadron's achievements and courage were recognised with honours and awards to 16 men, a ratio of almost one award for each ten men in the unit.

Major Peter Cameron, who commanded the squadron during the campaign, was awarded the Military Cross and the citation says that he led his squadron with humour and compassion both on the ground and in the air.

"His fine example of courage and determination, in the face of severe losses, was an inspiration to all and his leadership ensured that no call for help went unanswered," says the citation.

The squadron played a vital role in the campaign and in 12 weeks flew a total of well over 2,000 hours, more than three times its normal flying rate.

Weather limitations were ignored during the campaign. If it was humanly possible to fly, squadron pilots would be there to take out casualties and provide vital ammunition.

A classic casevac (casualty evacuation) sortie was flown by the Scout flight commander, Capt. Jeff Niblett, of Sidmouth. He twice attempted to go forward at night in thick mist to reach a young Royal Marine, who had lost a foot in a minefield.

The appalling conditions defeated him, but, at dawn, he took off again and spent a tense half an hour hover-taxi-ing forward in thick cloud to reach the injured man.

Limitations on loads also went by the board. In Gazelle pilot Lt. Bill Scott's words: "We just kept pulling at the stick to see if the aircraft would come up. If not, we threw off a box and tried again."

On D-Day, the squadron was immediately in action with the Special Boat Service in defeating the enemy at Fanning Head, moving key parties from one area to another, sometimes under fire.

Its little aircraft played a crucial role in establishing the bridgehead around San Carlos water, particularly in checking that sites intended for Rapier anti-aircraft missile posts were clear of the enemy.

It was during this phase that retreating enemy shot down a Gazelle, which was escorting a Sea King helicopter. After a brilliantly executed engine off landing in the sea, the two crew escaped from the ditched Gazelle.

The pilot, Sgt. Andy Evans, of Landrake, had been mortally wounded in the chest and stomach in the initial burst of machine-gun fire.

He and his crew, Sgt. E.R. Candlish, then came under fire again while swimming to the shore. The shots came from the same enemy, who had earlier hit the Gazelle. Incredibly, they were not hit and reached the shore after 20 minutes in ice cold water.

Falkland Islanders joined Sgt. Candlish in a desperate bid to save Sgt. Evan's life, but he died ten minutes after reaching the shore.

During follow-up operations against the retreating enemy, a second Gazelle was shot down. The pilot, Lt. Ken France, and his crew, Lance Corporal Pat Griffin, were both killed. The three Royal Marines fliers killed that first day of the landings were buried at sea from Canberra on the evening of May 22.

Captain Robin Makeig-Jones was the pilot of a third Gazelle hit by enemy fire on D-Day. His crewman was Corporal Roy Fleming. They were ordered to locate enemy troops, who had fired at a Sea King helicopter.

"On a second attempt to find them, I surprised them and they opened up with small arms, including machine-guns," said Capt. Makeig-Jones.

"They were in deep shadow and the sun was in my eyes. I was doing a dirty dash between cover when they opened up. The tail rotor was hit and a round came up through the cockpit from beneath because I was tilted at quite an angle.

"If my observer had been sitting in his normal seat beside me, I think he would have

The Royal Marines helicopters, both 'Scouts' and 'Gazelles', were used for casualty evacuation. A Fitzroy casualty is pictured here being carried to the hospital area having been flown in from the battlefield.

lost a leg. The bullet passed about 2ft from where I was sitting.''

Capt. Makeig-Jones went on: "I saw tracer before we were hit, so I was in an evasive manoeuvre by the time the aircraft was being hit. Everything was working all right, although the vibration had increased. I was able to fly into dead ground and then back to our ship.

"I told brigade where the enemy were and they were taken out by the Paras. When we were hit, I knew what I had to do. I was not scared then, but I was scared afterwards when I realised how close things had been.

"I did not know at that time that two other helicopters and three men from the squadron had been lost."

Capt. Makeig-Jones said one bullet had passed within a whisker of vital hydraulic pipes. If they had been hit, the tail rotor would have been useless. On board the logistic landing ship Sir Galahad the damaged rotor was replaced and the Gazelle was flying again within two hours with masking tape over the bullet holes.

"After the first casualties, we wondered if this was how the war was going to progress,'' said Capt. Makeig-Jones, a Royal Artillery officer, who was later Mentioned in Despatches.

"It brings out the character in men when they have to go off in cold blood, knowing two out of three aircraft have been shot down and the third shot up.

"I have great respect for those who took off after me, knowing that the expectancy of life was not going to be very high judged on the first experience," said Capt. Makeig-Jones.

Corporal Fleming, 28, was manning a machine-gun in the back of the helicopter when it was hit. He is convinced he would have been shot in the legs if he had been in his usual seat.

"We did a run up the side of a river and went back down the other side," he said. "We rounded a knoll and started seeing tracer coming towards us. It did not click at first that we had been hit.

"The pilot turned the aircraft as fast as he could. They hit us as we flew away. The aircraft was shaking from the hit in the tail rotor. I was waiting for bullets to come through the back and hit me or the pilot.

"I could still see two lines of tracer going beside the aircraft. I could see bullets hitting the ground in front of us. The worst part was the aircraft shaking. We had a fair way to go back to the ship.''

Corporal Fleming said: "Back on board, the first thing I did was to look at the damage. I did not realise until then how much stick we had taken. I had a coffee and a cigarette. Then we learned we had lost two aircraft. I knew two of the aircrew very well. The news cut me in half.''

During the days after the landings, the squadron flew from dawn to well after dusk supporting British forces in the now infamous "Bomb alley". Several aircraft came under air attack, but all took successful evasive action.

Two Gazelles and two Scouts were then placed in direct support of 2 Para's attack on Darwin and Goose Green. For three days, the aircraft flew continuously taking ammunition forward and bringing casualties out. They were often under fire.

Lt. Nunn was flying forward to take out wounded after Lt.Col. "H" Jones had been hit, when his aircraft was shot down by a Pucara.

The citation for Lt. Nunn's posthumous DFC says that his Scout was attacked by two Pucara's without warning. They fired rockets and cannons.

"By great flying skill, Lt. Nunn evaded the first attack but on the second his aircraft was hit and destroyed,'' says the citation.

It goes on: "Lt. Nunn displayed exceptional courage, flying skill and complete devotion to duty in the face of the enemy. His achievements that day, supporting the battalion, were exceptional and were instrumental in the eventual victory."

The squadron supported units establishing themselves at Teal, Estancia and Mount Kent and was in the thick of it when 42 Commando, 45 Commando and 3 Para made a co-ordinated night attack on Mount Harriet, Two Sisters and Mount Longdon. It was a crucial battle for the British.

In 24 hours, squadron helicopters evacuated some 85 wounded in appalling weather and under fire. Capt. Andy Newcombe and his aircrewman, Corporal Richard Roughton, were airborne for over five hours one night taking out casualties and guiding forward Royal Navy Wessex helicopters carrying vital artillery ammunition.

Two Gazelles, with their pilots using night

vision goggles, flew well forward of British lines in a daring casevac mission to recover three badly wounded Special Air Service soldiers.

The two aircrews were Capt. Nick Pounds flying with Sgt. Bill O'Brien and Capt. Makeig-Jones flying with Sgt. Jim Capelle. They flew through driving snow at 50ft on this remarkable mercy mission to the north of Port Stanley.

The squadron worked hard right up to the surrender on June 14, flying ammunition and medical supplies to Royal Marines and Paras and taking out their casualties.

In a fitting climax, Scouts were able to use their SS11 missiles to knock out three enemy gun positions early on June 14 before the surrender.

The squadron was proud that one of its aircraft, flown by Lt.Cdr. Gervais Corryton, was the first British helicopter to land in Port Stanley after the surrender. It carried urgent medical supplies for Paras entering the town.

Major Cameron paid tribute to every member of the squadron and he stressed that what was achieved in the air was only possible because of the work of the ground crews. He said they had worked magnificently under very difficult conditions.

Looking back on the campaign, Capt. Makeig-Jones said: "Being a pilot, you flew from a base in a safe area into a battle which was going on. You did not know how far the battle had progressed since you left it.

"The most difficult thing was to judge the mood of a battle and put the ammunition down exactly where it was needed. Casualties were usually further back, but still under artillery fire. But taking ammunition forward to people who needed it, meant you had to trust the man talking to you over the radio.

"Nothing was clear cut. You didn't know anything for certain."

Capt. Makeig-Jones went on: "It all seems

Straight from the can! Basic refuelling at the Commando Air Squadron forward operating base at Teal Inlet.

so unreal now. Life goes on normally. But it has certainly changed my attitude towards life.

"Everything becomes that much more precious. You don't take anything for granted any more, especially when you think how lucky you were at times."

Corporal Fleming said: "It was frightening. But for me, like a lot of others, it was the first time I had been involved in a conflict like that. It was not until we started to pick up casualties and we saw men who had been wounded that it was really brought home.

"You did not realise the horrors of it until you saw the wounded. Another thing that brought it home to me was seeing the dead on Mount Longdon."

Lt. Colin Baulf, 24, joined the squadron in January, 1982, after completing his flying training. He said that many of the rules he had learned in training went by the board in the combat flying he found himself pitched into.

He talked of one particular casevac mission, with Corporal Richard Roughton as crew, when they picked up a Royal Marine severely wounded by shrapnel.

"He was in a bad way when we picked him up," said Lt. Baulf. "We had to land for Corporal Roughton to give him mouth to mouth rescitation when he stopped breathing. Eventually he died. That brought it home. A man dies on you and you feel you have failed. Corporal Roughton did a very good job trying to keep that man alive."

Lt. Baulf said that he had learned a lot during those weeks of arduous flying.

"The first day I found frightening," he said. "After that, you just accepted what was going on and kept going. The other thing was picking up Argentinian casualties.

"You looked at them and you looked at ours and you thought 'what is the difference'."

First Royal Marines ashore

A Royal Marine from 40 Commando celebrated his 18th birthday flat on his back in the hospital ship Uganda after being blown up by a mine in the closing stages of the battle for the Falklands.

Marine Wayne McGregor lost a foot, but he said: "I feel I am lucky compared with others I saw."

40 Commando spearheaded the Royal Marines landing on the Falklands on May 21 and raised the Union Flag in San Carlos. The commando gradually assumed responsibility for the defence of the beach-head area and A and C Companies were sent to reinforce the Welsh Guards after their tragic losses at Fitzroy.

The anti-tank troop was attached to 45 Commando and saw service around Port Stanley. B Company and a composite company from Headquarters and Support Companies went with Lt.Col. Malcolm Hunt, commanding officer of 40 Commando, to West Falkland to receive the Argentinian surrender at Port Howard.

Men from 2 Para were first ashore at San Carlos on D-Day, but 40 Commando were only ten minutes behind them and dug in to prepare for a stay of, what everyone hoped would be, about a week.

Two men serving with 40 Commando, one of them a sapper from 59 Independent Commando Squadron, Royal Engineers, were killed in a bombing attack on May 27. Three other men were injured.

By then, other units were moving east in preparation for the assault on Port Stanley.

40 Commando hoped it would be relieved at the beach-head by a battalion from 5 Brigade and ordered to move east.

It was not to be and 40 Commando was ordered to remain where it was.

"It was a disappointment to us," said Lt.Col. Hunt. "We had been told we would be going east and staying behind was obviously disappointing."

The commando believed it might be ordered to relieve the Welsh Guards after the tragedy at Fitzroy when the landing ships Sir Galahad and Sir Tristram were devastated by air attacks. It was not to be, although A and C Companies from 40 Commando were moved to come under command of the Welsh Guards for the final battle.

Lieut. Carl Bushby, 23, a troop commander in C Company, has vivid memories of the battle by 42 Commando for Mount Harriet. The Welsh Guards with their reinforcements from 40 Commando had been ordered to secure the start line for 42 Commando's assault.

Moving in the dark over very difficult terrain with heavy loads meant the Guards were late arriving and the battle was in progress.

"We saw the battle for Mount Harriet," recalled Lieut. Bushby. "It was still dark, although it was a clear, moonlit night. We could see tracer and anti-tank rockets being fired and there was artillery support coming from behind us.

"There were star shells from the naval bombardment. There was a lot happening. It was like watching something from a war movie.

We were about one kilometre back from the action. We had mortar shells coming within 100 metres of our position. It seemed unreal.''

In another night operation, A and C Companies moved with the Welsh Guards to become the reserve for an attack on Mount William. During the move to a form-up point, they found themselves in a minefield.

The Guards and Royal Marines were moving in single file and many men had passed the spot where an anti-personnel mine suddenly blasted in the darkness and crippled Marine McGregor.

One theory to explain why the mine had not triggered earlier, was that the ground was frozen and the mine buried deep. The movement of troops over it might have loosened the earth enough for Marine McGregor to set the mine off with his boot.

''I was walking along when 'bang' and that was it,'' said Marine McGregor. ''I did not know how badly I was wounded. I knew I had

more than likely lost my foot. I was in great pain. I remember most of it.

''There was a loud bang. I saw a white flash between my legs and I was suddenly on my back facing the other way in a lot of pain.''

He went on: ''I remember the ride in the chopper. It took about 15 to 20 minutes. I had been given morphine which acted fairly quickly and took a lot of the pain away. It became a dull throb.''

Marine McGregor was first treated at the dressing station at Teal Inlet and then flown to the Uganda, where the remains of his shattered foot were amputated.

He was on Uganda for his 18th birthday on July 6 and was later taken to Montevideo on board HMS Hydra and flown home by the RAF to Brize Norton.

When Marine McGregor was injured, it was first thought the troops had come under mortar fire and they dived for cover. But minutes later Lieut. Paul Allen, a troop commander in

From day one, men of Commando Forces soon got used to the television cameras, who seemed to be constantly recording their every activity. Here men of A Company 40 Commando prepare to leave Plymouth.

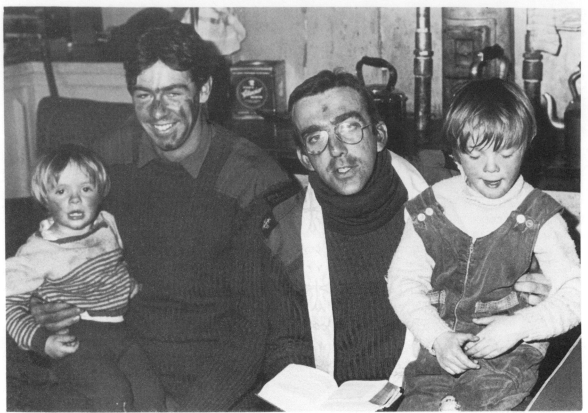

40 Commando's chaplain, Rev Godfrey Hilliard used a glass fruit bowl as a font when he baptized two children at San Carlos 2 days after D-Day. Lt. Mike Acland (left) of 40 Commando is godfather to both.

C Company, was injured by another mine and also lost a foot.

Royal Engineers were called forward to clear a route to the front and the advance continued. Ironically, the troops were later ordered back and the distance that had taken them seven hours during the advance took them only a fraction of the time to cover on the return.

A and C Companies were then deployed by helicopter to assault Sapper Hill early on June 14, the day the Argentinians surrendered. Lieut. Bushby's troop was landed in the wrong position.

"We were put down about 6 kilometres further east than we should have been," he said. "We left the helicopter under fire from Argentinian positions. It was mainly automatic fire from, I would say, about 20 enemy in hills some 200 metres to our front."

The Royal Marines took what little cover was available and began returning fire. They called for artillery support, but were unable to make radio contact with the gunners.

Marine Vince Comb, 17½ and the youngest man in the troop, was the machine-gunner and was hit by bullets in the wrist and arm. He was immediately replaced on the machine-gun and two Royal Marines gave him morphine and first aid.

About 20 minutes later, Lieut. Bushby was in communication with the rest of C Company and was told there were white flags over Port Stanley.

Sporadic fire followed, but the enemy was already withdrawing and a battalion position was later established on Sapper Hill. It was all over, bar the mine-clearing.

Lieut. Bushby said: "I would do it again. But I hope we never have to."

He talked of the great value of the Royal Marines tough training on Dartmoor and of the tremendous spirit throughout the unit.

The day after the Argentinian surrender was received by Major-General Jeremy Moore in Port Stanley, Lt.Col. Hunt flew over to West Falkland to accept the surrender there. He dealt with an Argentinian colonel and described the process as "all very gentlemanly".

Captain Stephen Bush, officer commanding B Company said the Royal Marines were kept busy that first day dealing with 850 Argentinian prisoners. Among them were about 18 whom medical officers assessed as not having eaten for at least two weeks. It was assumed their deprivation had been a punishment.

They were begging for food and one man was so weak he could hardly lift a spoon to his mouth.

"The majority of the Argentinians were relieved to see the end of the war," said Captain Bush. "Some of them were apprehensive about what was going to happen to them."

Captain Bush recalled his horror when he saw an Argentinian sick bay at Port Howard in West Falkland.

"It was in the most revolting condition you could imagine, with a rusty operating table and a cupboard containing clothing covered in congealed, dried blood. There was a bullet hole through the back of the clothing," said Captain Bush.

The settlement manager, concerned to protect the welfare of the local people, had agreed to supply the hungry Argentinians with a number of sheep each day.

Captain Bush said he learned that some of the Argentinians were so hungry they would eat sheep meat raw when they collected the carcasses. He was told there had been a scrabble for the sheep skulls, still with the wool attached.

In many Argentinian slit trenches, which Royal Marines filled in before they left Port Howard, they found sheep skulls picked clean.

The Royal Marines tried to restore normal-

Early days . . . men of 40 Commando in defensive positions around San Carlos settlement.

40 Commando took the surrender in West Falkland. The long job of searching prisoners begins.

The Union Flag—and 40 Commando's own are hoisted in West Falkland for the first time.

ity to Port Howard and Captain Bush said: "Our boys did a fantastic job."

Minefields were cleared and the British troops found oil drums on the beach filled with a deadly "cocktail" of anti-tank mines and rocks, with command wires leading away from them. Clearing the mines was made difficult because Argentinian military engineers were unsure of exact locations and numbers of mines.

Another Argentinian "refinement" discovered by the Royal Marines was anti-tank mines laid with trip wires in an anti-personnel role. In all, nearly 1,200 mines were cleared. Sadly, just before 40 Commando boarded Canberra for the voyage home, Corporal Trevor Lee, of B Company's assault engineer section, lost a foot when he stepped on an anti-personnel mine.

Lt.Col. Hunt said: "It was an extraordinary experience to be part of an operation like this, which was probably unique. Things did go wrong and one was sometimes worried about the eventual outcome.

"But I think most of us felt, as soon as we had landed, that there was no doubt about the outcome. It was an extraordinary operation to have been part of.

"My lasting impression is of the young men. They did a magnificent job. In spite of order and counter-order, which must happen in war, they maintained extraordinarily high morale.

"The morale and spirit of the unit was better than any I have ever known in 25 years service. They always came up smiling and always attacked whatever they had to do with the utmost dedication. They were magnificent."

Lt.Col. Hunt added: "Our training is right. It showed that the young men of today, if trained properly and disciplined, will be magnificent."

The Argentinians left a few surprises behind in West Falkland. Explosives and boulders packed in a steel drum needed careful handling.

Corporal Trevor Lee inspects mines he has cleared at Port Howard. Tragically, the next day, just hours before leaving for home, he lost a foot when a mine exploded.

Time to celebrate. Royal Marines are only too pleased to "splice the mainbrace" in a toast to the new-born Prince William.

Lt. Col. Malcolm Hunt, who led 40 Commando, recounts some of his unit's exploits to Prince Charles on their return home.

Food, glorious food. A human chain of Commandos hump their food ashore at Ajax Bay.

Atlantic Conveyor – The civilians' story

Two Devonport Dockyard men, who left their desks to sail with the Falklands Task Force, were on board the container ship Atlantic Conveyor when it was devastated by an Exocet missile.

Fire quickly raged out of control and the order was given to abandon ship. Mr Howard Ormerod and Mr Ron Edgecombe went over the side in survival suits and swam to the frail safety of a liferaft.

They were later taken aboard the frigate HMS Alacrity. Twelve of their shipmates from Atlantic Conveyor lost their lives, including the master, Captain Ian North.

Mr Ormerod, 29, an assistant supply and transport officer with the Royal Naval Supply and Transport Service, and Mr Edgecombe, 56, a stores officer with the RNSTS, were among the fifteen men in lounge suits who marched proudly through Plymouth in the city's welcome home parade.

Like all the 250 members of the RNSTS in Task Force ships they had earned the right to wear the South Atlantic medal and to march with the men-at-arms from the campaign.

Atlantic Conveyor was hastily converted in Devonport Dockyard for her war-time role. A flight deck was fitted to enable her to carry Chinook and Wessex helicopters and Harrier jets to the South Atlantic.

Mr Ormerod and Mr Edgecombe joined the ship at very short notice. Both had been to sea before with the Royal Fleet Auxiliary.

The voyage to Ascen-

One ship—two captains. Captain Ian North (left) and Captain Michael Layard on the bridge of Atlantic Conveyor. Captain North was lost after his ship was abandoned.

sion Island and then on south towards the Falklands were busy days for Atlantic Conveyor's men. Her Harriers had left her and she was steaming to unload her stores and helicopters in San Carlos when her war came to an end late on May 25.

Early that morning, Mr Edgecombe was in Atlantic Conveyor's dining room when he heard Captain North say to those near him: "Well boys, it's May 25. Something spectacular should happen today."

"Little did he realise it was his ship and his own life that were going to be lost," said Mr Edgecombe.

"During the day, it was a hive of activity down below as stores were prepared for off-loading. It was coming up towards evening meal time and we decided to break off for the first call for dinner.

"I had gone to my cabin to get ready and then went down to the dining room," recalled Mr Edgecombe. "I got my soup and sat down looking forward to a roast dinner. I had not got the first spoonful of soup down when the emergency alarm went."

Mr Ormerod said: "I was having a quick wash in my cabin. I heard the tannoy warning 'air raid alert red', which meant a raid was imminent. I went immediately to my emergency station, as I had done many times before.

"I had got to my station in the officers' bar when two things happened. Someone shouted 'hit the deck'. I was on my way to the floor when there was an almighty crash.

"I thought we had been hit by a bomb. That was what flashed through my mind," said Mr Ormerod.

Mr Edgecombe was also in the officers' bar and he remembers the order to hit the deck being followed by a big explosion.

"I remember saying 'what the hell was that?'," said Mr Edgecombe. "She was a big ship and we did not know at that stage where she had been hit or what by. Smoke started coming through the ventilation system quite soon."

Mr Ormerod said: "Very soon after, we lost

The beginning . . . Atlantic Conveyor prepares to sail from Plymouth Sound.

The end . . . 24 hours after an Exocet attack the charred remains shortly before she slipped beneath the waves.

communications both over the tannoy and by telephone. It was a big problem in a situation like that. We could smell fire and smoke very quickly and by then smoke was coming into the accommodation areas.

"We still did not know what had hit us. We knew we had been hit and that we were on fire. But we did not know what had hit us or where."

Word reached the officers' bar that the fire had taken hold in the main cargo deck. The men tried to go to strengthen the fire-fighting party, but they were driven back by dense smoke.

Mr Edgecombe and Mr Ormerod then tried to go forward to fetch stretchers, but were driven back by smoke.

"Visibility was down to about two yards, even out on deck, and the smoke was getting thicker," said Mr Ormerod. "Because of the lack of communications, we were not certain what was going on. We did not know whether there had been any injuries or whether the fire was gaining. We did not know at that

stage about the death of one of the engineers."

The two RNSTS men eventually located a stretcher locker in the accommodation area and took stretchers to the doctor in the dining room.

Mr Ormerod then decided to go to the bridge to report that there were places where the ship's deck was getting hot.

"We had been told by then that we had been hit by an Exocet missile," said Mr Edgecombe. "The missile had come into the cargo decks on the port quarter aft. You could not see the actual damage, only dense smoke coming up. There was the sound of stores exploding below."

Mr Edgecombe said that HMS Alacrity had been alongside playing hoses on the ship, but the warship had been forced to move away because of the danger of Atlantic Conveyor exploding. As she did so, Alacrity damaged some of the rope ladders hanging down the container ship's side.

The men on Atlantic Conveyor scrambled

into their survival suits when they were told to prepare to abandon ship. They moved to their liferaft stations. The order to leave the ship soon followed.

"I climbed down a rope ladder," said Mr Edgecombe. "I was part-way down. I felt for the next rung, but there was nothing there. I knew I could not go up because others were coming down. There was only one way to go and that was down. I let go and dropped about 15ft into the sea.

"I swam to a liferaft. It was full up and I was told to find another raft. There were enough rafts around. But I remember the feeling of reaching the first raft, feeling safe and then having to find another raft."

Mr Edgecombe said: "I suppose I was in the water 15 to 20 minutes by the time I got into a raft. We were still attached to the ship. You could hear explosions in the ship. There was a lot of smoke."

He added: "The calmness of the whole thing was incredible. No-one shouted or panicked. It was just like another exercise. Sometimes I find it hard to believe it really happened."

Mr Ormerod said: "It was a drop of about 40ft to the sea. We tried to climb as far as possible down a rope ladder. About half-way down the ladder had been carried away. The last 20ft or so was almost like scrambling down a single rope.

"I climbed down to about 10ft above the water and then jumped towards a liferaft. I swam towards the raft, but a wave brought the raft right on top of me. It was the worst moment for me.

"I was right beneath the centre of the raft. For a few horrible seconds, I was in dark water. I swam on my back underwater to get clear.

"When I got clear, another wave took the liferaft away from me. I swam towards another raft and, luckily, I made it. There was one man in the raft and he helped me get into it. We then helped about 15 men to get aboard."

Mr Ormerod went on: "The next thing was to get across to Alacrity. We had cut the raft free from Atlantic Conveyor. Alacrity fired gun lines and we managed to grab two of them and pull ourselves towards her."

Once alongside the frigate, the men in Mr Ormerod's raft waited their turn to climb scrambling nets to the safety of Alacrity's deck.

"I went up the scrambling net like a rat up a drainpipe and when I got to the top I was absolutely shattered," said Mr Ormerod.

Mr Edgecombe, who was in another liferaft, hurt his back when he was holding a rope from Alacrity and a large wave lifted his raft and threw him violently back inside it. He was winched up to the frigate's deck in a harness.

"It was marvellous to get on Alacrity," said Mr Edgecombe. "We were soon below and out of our wet clothing. The cold had just started to get to us."

Both men were invited to go to Alacrity's bridge for a last look at Atlantic Conveyor. "She looked like a gigantic firework display," said Mr Ormerod. "You could see the outline of the ship and where the fires were."

Next day, some of the dead from Atlantic Conveyor were buried at sea from Alacrity and on May 27 the survivors were transferred to the tanker British Tay for the voyage to Ascension and a flight home to RAF Brize Norton.

Mr Edgecombe, who had only praise for Alacrity, went to meet the frigate when she arrived home in Devonport. With him went a couple of bottles of champagne for the chiefs' mess where he had been made so welcome after being rescued.

His son, Stephen, 30, is a Customs officer and was one of the team which cleared Alacrity when she arrived home. It gave him the chance to say a personal "thank you" to the ship's company for saving his father.

Mr Edgecombe's wife, Margaret, said she was with a friend when she was told Atlantic Conveyor had been hit but that her husband was one of the survivors.

"Thank God I was saved the anxiety of switching on the television and seeing the news before I had been told," said Mrs Edgecombe. "Nothing else matters any more except that my husband came back safely. I have a different outlook on life as a result of this. My prayers were answered."

Mr Edgecombe said: "One of our biggest disappointments was that we did not complete what we went down there to do. And there was the sadness of losing shipmates and our ship down there.

"I feel I am very lucky. I feel proud to wear the South Atlantic medal and to have been part of the operation."

Atlantic Conveyor after the missile struck.

Mr Ormerod said it was frustrating to have got so close to the Falklands without being able to complete the job they had set out to do.

"People say 'you got sunk', but there is no credit given to the ship for what she did," said Mr Ormerod. "We got the Harriers off and we had transferred a fair amount of aircraft equipment to other ships.

"We had also transferred a lot of stores to other ships on the way down and at Ascension. We had got rid of the vast majority of the transit stores for other units before we were hit."

Mr Ormerod's then girl friend, Liz, a QARNNS senior nursing officer from Plymouth's Royal Naval Hospital, was serving in the hospital ship Uganda.

"All the way down, I told our helicopter pilots that, as soon as we got within range of Uganda, I was going to drop something on my foot to get injured or persuade them to fly me across to see Liz," said Mr Ormerod.

"Alacrity signalled the names of the survivors she picked up the Commander-in-Chief Fleet and the message that I was safe reached Liz. When I got home, she phoned me from Uganda. I asked her to marry me."

Mrs Ormerod said: "I was told Atlantic Conveyor had been lost at about 8 am the day after she was hit. It was about 18 hours before I learned that Howard was among the survivors.

"We were so busy in the Uganda that I just got on with it. But it was difficult to rest off duty until I heard he was safe. I felt the next lot of casualties might include him.

"The Senior Naval Officer in Uganda eventually came to tell me Howard was all right. All the signal said was that he had no significant injury.

"We had talked about getting married before I went away. When I phoned Howard from the ship, we decided the wedding should be sooner rather than later."

Night Attack

Lt.Col. Nick Vaux D.S.O. R.M. Commanding Officer 42 Commando.

A brilliantly-executed silent night attack from behind enabled 42 Commando to surprise 500 Argentinians holding a vital mountain strong-point only a few miles from Port Stanley.

The attack on Mount Harriet saw bitter close-quarter combat for several hours, but the Royal Marines of 42 Commando secured their objective with the loss of only one man and a number of wounded.

Up to 50 Argentinians were killed in the fierce fighting, 300 were taken prisoner and the rest fled in confusion.

The battle for Mount Harriet was part of Brigadier Julian Thompson's carefully co-ordinated silent attack by 3rd Commando Brigade on the night of June 12. 3 Para took Mount Longdon in a bloody fight, 45 Commando seized Two Sisters and 42 Commando swept to victory among the rocks and crags of Mount Harriet.

It was the decisive land action of the campaign. It saw the Argentinians driven demoralised and in confusion from three crucial mountain strongholds. British victory was assured as the stranglehold tightened remorselessly on the main Argentinian force in Port Stanley.

The plan to attack Mount Harriet "through the back door" was the idea of Lt.Col. Nick Vaux, who commanded 42 Commando. He was able to carry out his surprise attack, described as "a brilliant piece of work" by Brig. Thompson, only after nights of hazardous patrolling by his men.

Routes had to be charted through the mine-fields around Mount Harriet and two young Royal Marines had their legs shattered by mines during the long hours of patrolling. Fighting patrols deliberately provoked Argentinian fire so that enemy strong-points, particularly heavy machine-guns, could be pin-pointed.

The battle for Mount Harriet came only two days before the Argentinian surrender and it was a remarkable achievement for the Green Beret men from Bickleigh, near Plymouth. They had lived for three weeks in appalling conditions, soaked most of the time and with little shelter from gales and rain.

Stark contrast to the conditions they enjoyed in the liner Canberra on the voyages to and from the Falklands.

When Lt.Col. Vaux gave the now famous command "To the South Atlantic, quick march" at Bickleigh Barracks early in April, he knew that M Company was already earmarked for the operation to seize South Georgia back from the Argentinians. His second-in-command, Major Guy Sheridan, led that highly successful operation, which saw the Argentinians run up the first of their white flags.

On the voyage south, J Company was formed to fill the gap left by M Company. It was fitting that it should be commanded by Major Mike Norman, who had led the defence of Government House in Port Stanley just a few weeks earlier.

He and men from Naval Party 8901, who had been forced to surrender to the invaders through overwhelming odds, had eagerly volunteered to return to the fight. They and men from a number of elements in 42 Commando made up the new J Company now disbanded.

It was about a week after D-Day at San Carlos that 42 Commando was ordered to make a night assault on Mount Kent as the British move east to Port Stanley began.

Appalling weather meant the postponement of the operation, but a second attempt saw the Royal Marines airlifted into position by helicopter. The SAS were already on Mount Kent and 42 Commando settled down to reconnaissance and fighting patrols in the build-up to the assault on Mount Harriet.

The commandos dug in where possible and used their ponchos and rocks and boulders to create some shelter from the elements.

"We quickly discovered we were much better at night fighting than the Argentinians," said Lt.Col. Vaux. "Clearly they were very inexperienced."

"We became aware tragically and very quickly that the enemy on Mount Harriet had minefields which seemed to extend almost all the way around the mountain."

Marines Mark Curtis and Kevin Paterson had legs shattered by mines.

"One man was carried for ten hours and only survived through the skill of Leading Medical Assistant Heywood and the dedication of his chums, who carried him across horrendous terrain, much of the time under shellfire," said Lt.Col. Vaux.

He said that one of the injured men was airlifted for medical treatment by a Gazelle helicopter from the Commando Brigade Air Squadron under fire and in some of the most dangerous night flying conditions he had ever seen.

Lt.Col. Vaux paid tribute to Sgt. Jumper Collins for his patrol work, which played a vital part in gathering intelligence for the attack on Mount Harriet.

Sgt. Collins, 29, was awarded the Military Medal. He led two hazardous patrols to find

Battle planning as 42 Commando make plans in the cleft of a rock using an improvised model of Mount Harriet.

No time to shave—men of J Company 42 Commando, who were in the original tiny Falklands garrison prepare for the big push back to their old barracks.

paths through minefields and a covered approach to the intended start line for the attack.

Marine Paterson was in one of Sgt. Collins' patrols when he lost a foot in a mine explosion. Sgt. Collins used his hands and a bayonet to feel for mines as he led the men carrying the injured Royal Marine to safe ground.

He handed the casualty to another senior NCO and his men—and returned to continue the vital work of probing the route for the forthcoming attack. Lt.Col. Vaux asked Sgt. Collins to return on a second night patrol behind enemy lines to confirm the attack route and locate the start line.

"It was very apparent to me that all their defences, which were very significant and included a lot of heavy machine-guns, were sited towards Goose Green to cover the road to Port Stanley," said Lt.Col. Vaux.

"We were directly opposite them. I did not want to be forced into their killing ground by attacking from that direction."

Intelligence from his patrols enabled him to plan his attack from behind Mount Harriet, with a diversionary attack to make the Argentinians believe a frontal assault was in progress.

J Company was chosen to create the diversion as L and K companies slipped silently into position for the real attack. Dummy mines were set off, shots rang out and men screamed as J Company sought to convince the Argentinians an attack was coming from the front.

Heavy machine-guns in high rocks were a major threat and the diversionary attack was used to coax the Argentinians into firing them. The Commandos then retaliated with anti-tank rockets, which knocked out some of the machine-gun nests.

L and K Companies moved safely through the minefield and swung round behind Mount

Harriet. K Company was not detected until it was only 50 metres from enemy positions. The fight was on and it was at close quarters.

"Once we got into the fighting, we all switched to 'auto' and got stuck in," said Sgt. Collins. "The guys worked fantastically. We were fighting the enemy at five and ten metres. We were literally knocking their weapons from the hands and going on."

Sgt. Collins was fighting alongside Corporal Laurence Watts who was killed when they assaulted an enemy position.

"He went to the left and I went to the right," said Sgt. Collins. "He called grenade because he was going to throw one. The Argentinians fired and he fell wounded."

Cpl. Watts was dead when Sgt. Collins reached him.

Describing the battle, Sgt. Collins said: "You came round a rock and fired. We yelled and talked to each other all the time."

Marine Mark Wallace, 18, said: "I was quite surprised when we started going up Mount Harriet. One of our corporals opened fire and they opened up with a heavy machinegun. It all went from there."

"I felt most scared at the beginning. Once we got into the swing of the battle, the old adrenalin got going and it was not too bad."

"I remember a bloke put up his head to shoot at me from about 50 metres. I fired at him. There was a fair bit of close quarter work. I was shot at a few times. You don't think about it at the time. I was frightened. But the training paid off."

Lance-Corporal Paul Basford, 20, said: "We did not have time to think. There was not much fear involved until we got to the top and then we realised what was happening.

"I must have fired about 150 rounds from my machine-gun, mostly at flashes from enemy guns. You could see their positions

Training on Dartmoor pays off. The terrain is similar, but this time it is for real as men of K Company 42 Commando patrol Mount Kent.

Three cheers for the choppers. 42 Commando's mortar troop took a "cab" to Mount Kent.

because they used tracer. I had it close, but I was not hit."

Lance-Cpl. Basford added: "I would not like to do it again. There was a lot of running forward and hitting the deck because you couldn't run through the fire they were putting up."

Marine Geoff Inwood, 18, said: "It is difficult to describe. There was firing all the time. I thought I had been hit, but I found a shot had gone through the water bottle on my hip. Much later, I found the round had gone through and lodged inside my windproof jacket.

"There was just relief when it was all over."

By first light on June 13, 42 Commando had secured Mount Harriet and linked up with 45 Commando on Two Sisters.

"Considering the position and strength of the defences, we were very lucky," said Lt.Col. Vaux.

He spoke of the vital support given throughout by the gunners from 29 Commando Regiment, Royal Artillery, which is based at Plymouth's Royal Citadel. Two gunner officers, Capt. Chris Romberg and Capt. Nick Dapucci, acted as forward observers directing the artillery fire.

"We were so confident in their skill that we let them call fire within 50 to 100 metres of our own troops," said Lt.Col. Vaux. "You really have to have faith to do that.

"I spoke to a wounded Argentinian officer and he told me the most decisive factor at Mount Harriet, apart from the attack coming from behind, was the artillery fire," said Lt.Col. Vaux.

He added: "It was amazing to me that young marines, who had finished training only in the past year or so, were able to be so cool and professional in sustaining the momentum in those circumstances. We were very lucky."

Lt.Col. Vaux spoke of the professionalism

Wet and dishevelled an Argentinian soldier is searched by Sgt Alan Starling of 42 Commando.

Time for a joke. Lt.Col. Nick Vaux talks to some of his men. He is seen right with rifle.

of the British troops at all levels. "They understood they must close with the enemy and keep going. They knew they must not get bogged down and allow the enemy to regroup."

42 Commando consolidated on Mount Harriet and nearby Goat Ridge and Lt.Col. Vaux said: "It was marvellous. You could see Port Stanley. One knew victory was not far away."

He recalled: "It was fearfully cold. We really looked like the most original crowd of mountain bandits you have ever seen."

His commando prepared for more action, but the surrender was soon to come.

Lt.Col. Vaux said he believed Arctic training in Norway had been invaluable. He underlined the very difficult conditions his commandos had lived through before the battle for Mount Harriet.

On the return voyage in Canberra, medical staff found 97 per cent of K Company suffering from some form of trench foot as a legacy of the long weeks of cold, wet conditions.

"The endurance of the young marines was unexpectedly dogged," said Lt.Col. Vaux. "It is a British quality. We still have it. They simply would not give up. The morale and the determination never wavered. They were determined to go on and finish the job."

He added: "There were some bad times and some very frightening moments. There were some bad moments when one might have thought were we going to get it right and win.

"But you only had to look around for the answer. The men were simply not going to be beaten. Their morale was the decisive factor."

HMS Antelope – The final hours

A 20mm Oerlikon gun, used to shoot down an Argentinian plane attacking HMS Antelope, was salvaged after the frigate sank and mounted on her sister-ship, HMS Avenger. It was dubbed "Antelope's Avenger".

Antelope and another Type 21 frigate, HMS Ardent, were both lost through the savage air attacks mounted by the Argentinians after the British landings in the Falklands.

Two 1,000 lb bombs hit Antelope, but both failed to explode. Tragically, one of the bombs was triggered during attempts to defuse it and the ship was torn open and set on fire by the huge explosion.

Antelope's captain, Commander Nick Tobin, talked of the air attacks and the loss of his ship.

D-Day at San Carlos had been on May 21 and Antelope steamed into an air defence station at the entrance to San Carlos Water early on May 23.

"The idea was to put a cork in the bottle and bottle up the entrance to San Carlos Water so that attacking aircraft would have to fly over us and through our anti-aircraft barrage before they could get to the bulk of the amphibious ships in San Carlos Water," said Cdr. Tobin.

Antelope's 4.5 inch automatic gun, Seacat missiles, two Oerlikon guns and machine-guns were able to put up a formidable hail of fire.

She was hit about four hours after she moved into position, but before that her Lynx helicopter had attacked and damaged a 6,000-ton Argentinian freighter further to the south.

The pilot, Lt. Timothy McMahon, and his observer, Lt. Gary Hunt, returned south a couple of hours later to reassess the damage to the freighter. The Lynx's two Sea Skua missiles had caused considerable damage.

The Lynx was flying back to Antelope when Lt. MacMahon realised he was locked on to by a hostile control radar. He dropped down to about 40ft and increased to maximum speed.

"Almost at the same time, he was overflown by four Argentinian Skyhawks flying north up Falkland Sound," said Cdr. Tobin. "Lt. MacMahon reported these aircraft. We had previous indications that an air attack was on its way.

"Lt. Jonathan Sharp and other members of the bridge personnel saw four aircraft fly across the mouth of San Carlos Water and disappear behind a headland. We had been at action stations since dawn and we were prepared for an attack.

"In what seemed like seconds, but was probably a couple of minutes, we were attacked by two aircraft which came down from the north over the sky line. They dived down the side of a hill and flew very low towards us."

Cdr. Tobin went on: "One plane came straight at us. He dropped two bombs and he was engaged by my starboard 20mm Oerlikon gun, which was aimed and fired by Leading Seaman "Bunny" Warren.

"The aircraft was about 30ft above the water and flying very fast. One bomb flew between the mainmast and the foremast and the other hit the ship on the starboard side aft.

"The aircraft was hit by about eight shells from Leading Seaman Warren's gun. It pulled up, hit the mainmast and disintegrated in a big ball of flame, scattering debris about 100 yards from the ship."

Cdr. Tobin said: "Leading Seaman Warren said he aimed and closed his eyes as the plane got close, but he kept on firing. It was his shells that destroyed the aircraft. The mast of the ship gave the coup de grace.

"It was rather fitting that Antelope should spear the plane with one of her horns."

Because she was so close to land, Antelope, in common with other ships in her position, could not use her primary gunnery control system and her men had to fire by eye. They were getting only five or six seconds from seeing an attacking plane to engaging it.

Just after she was hit by the first bomb, Antelope was attacked by two more aircraft coming in from the port side.

"We opened up with the 4.5 inch gun and the Seacat," said Cdr. Tobin. "The two planes turned away and a Seacat missile chased one of them up a nearby ridge. We believe it destroyed the aircraft just over the ridge.

"We were then attacked again from our port side and a bomb entered the ship forward in the vicinity of the petty officers' mess. The attacks during which we were hit, were made within about one minute and it was evident they were co-ordinated and very professionally carried out."

The first bomb had struck aft just above Antelope's two engine rooms. The second had killed Steward Mark Stephens, aged 18, and injured two other ratings.

Leading Stores Accountant Paul Ridge suffered a fractured skull, but later recovered. Stores Assistant Kerr was less seriously hurt.

"It was all very quick," recalled Cdr. Tobin. "There were lots of guns firing and missiles being fired. There was the chattering of the machine guns and the slightly slower chatter of the Oerlikons. A lot of lead was in the air.

"I was in the operations room and I went immediately to the bridge and saw the remnant of the raid flying north. The bombs had caused quite a lot of damage and casualties, but neither had exploded."

Two Army bomb disposal experts, Warrant Officer Phillips and Staff Sgt Jim Prescott, were later embarked to deal with the bombs on board. The ship's company were moved as far away as possible and Lt.Cdr. Richard Goodfellow and CPO Porter remained with the bomb disposal experts.

"WO Phillips and Staff Sgt Prescott were confident they would do the job," said Cdr Tobin. "They started with the bomb aft and said they had only recently dealt with a similar bomb in another ship.

"It was now well after dark. They had made several attempts to defuse the bomb using various methods. It exploded during another attempt and blew a huge hole in the ship's side from the water-line to the funnel."

The blast started major fires in both engine rooms and the fires spread very quickly. Staff Sgt Prescott was killed in the explosion and WO Phillips lost an arm. Lt.Cdr. Goodfellow and CPO Porter escaped with minor injuries and shock.

The ship's company was mustered aft on the flight deck and Cdr. Tobin instructed his First Lieutenant, Lt.Cdr. Robert Guy, to go aft and see what he could do to save the ship.

"We tried for about an hour to fight the fires and contain the damage, but it was rapidly becoming a losing battle," said Cdr. Tobin.

Many vital systems, including the fire-main and all electrical supplies, had been lost and the fires spread out of control.

"I was cut off on the bridge with six others," said Cdr. Tobin. "There was thick acrid smoke being fanned by a headwind of 15 to 20 knots, which was making life untenable for the ship's company on the flight deck.

"It soon became apparent the ship would have to be abandoned. I had lost communications with the First Lieutenant. Separately, but at the same time, he and I ordered the ship to be abandoned. The ship's company were taken off by landing craft. My small team was picked up forward by landing craft.

"I think I was the last to leave her. I climbed down a knotted rope into a landing craft. I felt a sense of shock, probably more frustration than anything else. I felt cheated. It all happened so quickly. The boys were all very calm indeed."

Cdr. Tobin paid this tribute to his men: "In action they were superbly professional and

**FAREWELL TO
A FINE SHIP**

steady. I never once saw a man flinch or turn away or not do his duty to the best of his ability. I think the average age of my ship's company was about 21."

About five minutes after Antelope was abandoned, one of the missile magazines blew up. Ten minutes later the main missile magazine exploded.

Cdr. Tobin saw his ship sink next day. The night had seen more explosions aboard the blazing Antelope and in the morning Cdr. Tobin saw her back was broken.

"There were still great clouds of smoke. The ship was very blackened," he said. "There was a great billowing of white smoke and she finally broke her back completely and sank with the bow and stern sticking up out of the water in a 'V' shape.

"I thought at the time that it was a 'V' gesture of defiance. She sank completely later."

The dead remained in Antelope and a memorial to them and the dead in HMS Ardent has since been erected on Sussex Mountain overlooking their last resting places.

Cdr. Tobin said that his ship's company had been mortified when they heard of Ardent's loss two days before their own ship was hit.

"In some ways it made my people all the keener to join battle to avenge all our chums in Ardent," said Cdr. Tobin.

"Looking back, I feel a sense of pride in my ship's company for what they did all the way down to the Falklands and for what they were in action and subsequently.

"The psychological impact of losing the ship, losing friends and seeing friends injured is very great. I was proud of the way they handled the whole thing.

"Some people think the youth of today are not as good as the youth of their day. My ship's company was the finest bunch of young lads I have ever served with."

Cdr. Tobin added: "There is nothing special about them. They are young men who happen to have chosen the Royal Navy as a career. They are a product of the English character. A certain amount of pragmatism; good training and pride. It all combines to make some very good people."

He went on: "I think we did our job well. There was only a millimetre in it either way when the bomb was being defused. If it had been defused, we would have lived to fight throughout the operation. It was frustrating not to be able to complete the job I believe we started so well."

Commando Gunners

Three batteries of guns from 29 Commando Regiment, Royal Artillery, played a vital part in the battle for the Falklands, devastating enemy positions, supporting British assaults and helping crush Argentinian morale.

Brigadier Julian Thompson, who led 3rd Commando Brigade, said the three batteries from 29 Commando Regiment and two others from another regiment were, perhaps, the battle winning factor in the war.

"The ability to bring down concentrated, accurate fire crushed the enemy's morale and raised ours," said Brig. Thompson.

"Thanks to training on the passage down, every Royal Marine or private soldier learned how to call for fire and correct it; and many did so.

"Our gunners often brought down fire within 50 metres of our own troops in the attack. We had the utmost confidence in them."

Brig. Thompson continued: "Once again, artillery proved itself to be the principle man killing weapon in the land battle. If properly handled, which ours was, it is undeterred by smoke, darkness, snow or fog.

"It is accurate, almost instantaneous and devastating."

29 Commando Regiment, which has its headquarters at Plymouth's Royal Citadel, has three batteries of guns, each consisting of six 105 mm light guns.

The Falklands campaign was the first time these British built guns had been fired in anger. They can fire a 35 lb shell up to 17,000 metres with devastating accuracy.

The regiment has 148 Commando Forward Observation Battery, with the main task of providing observation ashore for naval gunfire support.

This battery was involved in clandestine operations with the SAS and Special Boat Section, when small parties were landed under cover of darkness to direct naval gunfire on to Argentinian targets.

For the Falklands campaign, T (Shah Sujah Troop) Air Defence Battery of 12 Air Defence Regiment, Royal Artillery, from Lincolnshire, was placed under 29 Commando Regiment's command. Its Rapier missiles claimed 13 confirmed "kills" of Argentinian planes and a number of probable "kills".

Lt.Col. Mike Holroyd-Smith, who commanded 29 Commando Regiment during the campaign, also took under his command a parachute gun battery from 4th Field Regiment, which supported 2 Para.

29 Commando Regiment was airlifted ashore by helicopter on May 21, D-Day for the British landings at San Carlos. With dawn not coming until late morning, it was a concentrated operation—40 helicopter lifts are needed to get one battery and its 60 tons of ammunition ashore.

"The greatest logistics problem of the whole operation was providing ammunition for the batteries and we never ran out," said Major Julian Starmer-Smith, second-in-command of 29 Commando Regiment.

"This is a tribute to the logistics people and

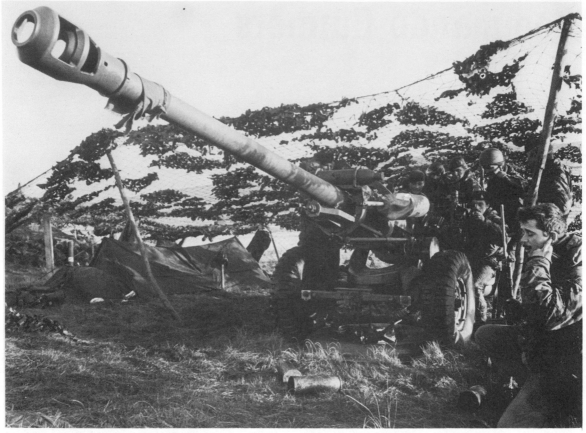

Plenty of Argentinians would like to forget the effect of 29 Commando Regiment's 105 mm guns.

to the pilots of 846 Squadron. We fired around 12,000 rounds during the campaign."

The regiment's first shells fired in anger silenced a machine-gun position, which had been troubling 42 Commando.

Then came the Darwin-Goose Green operation by 2 Para, which was supported by three guns from 8 (Alma) Battery. They were continuously in action during the bitter fighting.

Captain Kevin Arnold was serving with 148 Commando Forward Observation Battery during the Falklands campaign and he was part of the command group with 2 Para's commanding officer, Lt.Col. H. Jones, at Goose Green.

His party from 148 Battery was directing fighter ground attack and, towards the end of the battle, a final pocket of Argentinian resistance was causing heavy British casualties. The gunners were able to direct air strikes, which destroyed the enemy position.

Capt. Arnold was only about 100 yards from Col. Jones when he was killed and he and four other gunners from 148 Battery were very much involved in the fighting with their own small arms.

"It was frightening," said Capt. Arnold. "I think most people would say that, but because of the training we receive, you overcome it and, after a while, it faded into the background."

After the victory at Goose Green, guns from another of 29 Commando Regiment's batteries were flown to the Mount Kent area and operated for several days solely with units from the SAS. Slowly they were joined by the rest of the guns from the regiment and two batteries from another regiment in the build-up to the big push towards Port Stanley.

In a brilliantly co-ordinated silent night attack, 3 Para took Mount Longdon, 42 Commando secured Mount Harriet and 45

Commando took Two Sisters. The gunners from Plymouth with two batteries from 4th Field Regiment provided devastatingly accurate supporting fire. Gunfire from Royal Navy ships was directed by 148 Battery.

"We were firing non-stop," recalled Major Starmer-Smith. "Everyone was calling for fire. It went on throughout the night and we continued harassing fire on the enemy running away."

He said that one of the difficulties throughout the campaign was very soft, peaty ground into which the guns dug themselves with their recoil after firing about 20 rounds. The gunners then had to manhandle the guns to firm ground and re-align them to begin firing again.

"This was done at night in freezing cold," said Major Starmer-Smith. "Everyone worked extremely hard. It was shattering work for the gun detachments."

Normal gun detachments of six were swelled with anyone available to help with the back-breaking work of keeping the guns firing and humping heavy ammunition from pallets landed by helicopters.

During the three-battalion night attack, there was sporadic enemy artillery fire towards the British batteries, but the Argentinian gunners were without "eyes" because the British had seized all the high ground and there were no forward observers to direct enemy fire.

The following day, the gunners were re-supplied with ammunition and prepared to support 5 Brigade's attack on Tumbledown and Mount William. 2 Para took Wireless Ridge and the Scots Guards secured Tumbledown.

"As the enemy turned and ran, we were literally following them with shellfire to the outskirts of Port Stanley," said Major Starmer-Smith.

29 Commando Regiment came through the campaign almost unscathed, although some men received minor injuries from shrapnel and splinters during air attacks.

Ironically, the regiment's only serious casualty was injured when a mine exploded beneath a Volvo oversnow vehicle on the evening General Moore received the Argentinian surrender in Port Stanley.

Major Brian Armitage was taking radios to Port Stanley in a Volvo driven by Gunner Gordon Caren.

"We ran over a mine. I went up through the roof and the vehicle went up and was turned right round by the explosion," said Major Armitage, who broke his back in four places and suffered rib fractures.

"I landed about 15 metres from the vehicle. It took me a long time to start breathing again. I thought I was dying. I had broken my back before parachuting and I knew there was something very seriously wrong. I was hoping I would faint. The pain was excruciating," said Major Armitage.

"Gunner Caren came across to me and we went into a survival routine. He was not injured. It was cold and snowing. Our radios were smashed. We had to sit it out until help came 15 hours later.

"Gunner Caren got sleeping bags to cover me and then he made a cover for us

A crucial load, ammunition from Teal Inlet for the Gunners at Mount Kent—every load was desperately needed at the front.

with bits and pieces. Without his help I think I would have died from exposure."

Because they were in a minefield, Gunner Caren could only move with the greatest care between the spot where Major Armitage lay in agony and the wreckage of their Volvo—the force of the explosion had ripped the cab and trailer units apart. Next day, two men were seriously injured clearing the minefield.

"When we hit the mine, it was just as if someone had picked up the Volvo and thumped it down," recalled Gunner Caren. "I remember getting rattled around the cab and the major went straight out."

Major Armitage said: "I could not feel my legs or feet. The hours passed slowly."

He spent three months in hospital and ten weeks in a plaster cast. He was eventually able to return to the regiment.

Capt. Arnold said that he believed 148 Battery was lucky no one was killed or injured, particularly when parties went ashore on clandestine operations with the SAS and SBS to direct naval gunfire on to enemy targets.

"We were very lucky," he said. "We did not know where the enemy were in detail. Every time we went ashore we always had to be prepared to fight or withdraw."

Five parties from 148 Battery were involved in clandestine operations before the main landings on May 21 and after that the battery was involved in every operation until the surrender.

"Looking back I feel how lucky we were with our young men," said Capt. Arnold. "I consider myself very lucky to have led some of the high quality soldiers we have.

"It was a very difficult campaign in terms of the problems of weather, terrain and the logistic difficulties. But I believe our training made us more than capable of handling it."

One of the lighter moments in the serious business of the Falklands campaign has found a permanent place in the regiment's anecdotes. During a clandestine operation, a party put ashore by small boat took cover when indistinct figures were spotted at a distance in the dark.

They laid low for some time, prepared to fight, if necessary. The figures drew a little nearer in the darkness, only to be identified as penguins.

Major Starmer-Smith believes the regiment was very lucky during the campaign. "We had some very near misses, particularly with our forward observation parties. There has never been an operation like this as far as I am concerned.

"I am sure we played a decisive part in the campaign. Our fitness and training were really put to the test and came through very well. Our soldiers showed their ability to adapt to the conditions and to improvise. Morale was always absolutely sky-high."

He added: "I think the British Government sent the first eleven. They sent the fittest and most robust troops in the Commandos and Paras. The young men came out of it very well. I cannot think of anyone, who let the regiment down in any way during the whole campaign."

Broadsword and the bouncing bomb

Argentinian Skyhawk jets roared low across the water towards the frigate, HMS Broadsword, a few miles off the Falklands.

A bomb from one of them bounced off the waves, tore into the warship's side . . . ripped its way up through the flight deck . . . smashed the front off a Lynx helicopter—then fell harmlessly over the side without exploding!

Broadsword had led a charmed life in the thick of the action after the British landings at San Carlos and Lady Luck was still smiling on her.

Incredibly, no one was injured when the bomb struck and the ship's engineers were able to weld patches over the damage and keep the frigate in fighting trim for the rest of the campaign in the South Atlantic.

It was May 25 and it was the day luck ran out for the destroyer, HMS Coventry, with which Broadsword had teamed up for operations just off the islands.

Only minutes after the attack on Broadsword, the Skyhawks turned their attention on Coventry and bombs left the destroyer crippled and sinking rapidly. Broadsword picked up about 170 of the survivors.

Broadsword had sailed from Devonport on March 17 for a Mediterranean exercise and was scheduled to sail on to ports in the Persian Gulf, India and, finally, to Singapore.

She left Gibraltar on April 5 and was dramatically recalled and ordered to join the Falklands Task Force. Her main role until May 21 when the British landed at San Carlos was as "goal-keeper" for the carrier, HMS Hermes.

Lt.Cdr. Nigel Bray, an advanced warfare officer in Broadsword, explained that "goal-keeping" meant that Broadsword, whose armament included the Sea Wolf anti-missile missile, stayed close to Hermes to protect her from air attack.

"We spent week after week close to Hermes," said Lt.Cdr. Bray. "When the threat of attack was low, we were within about one mile. We were as close as 200 yards when the threat of attack was high."

"There were occasions between May 1 and 21 when, because of the monotony of our role, Admiral Woodward was kind enough to give us rather more exciting things to do."

Broadsword teamed up with Coventry to be her "goal-keeper" when the destroyer went in close to land to bombard shore targets and the frigate was involved in some hush-hush operations.

"We had three weeks of real monotony, punctuated with the odd exciting mission," said Lt.Cdr. Bray.

Broadsword, commanded during the campaign by Captain Bill Canning, was among the warships chosen to provide air defence for the D-Day landings at San Carlos.

The plan was to force the Argentinian pilots to fly through the warships' anti-aircraft fire before they could attack the ships putting men and stores ashore.

"Air raids started about half an hour after sunrise on May 21 and carried on until about half an hour before sunset," said Lt.Cdr. Bray.

In addition to its Sea Wolf missiles, which claimed one plane on the first day and a second in "bomb alley", Broadsword had a "secret" weapon.

This was an upper deck small arms battery, a mixed crew of sailors and Royal Marines, blasting away at Argentinian planes with a 40 mm Bofors gun, machine-guns and rifles. The team, led by Royal Marines Sergeant Bill Leslie, shot down two planes and damaged two more.

Sgt. Leslie was awarded the Distinguished Service Medal. Some of the upper deck sharpshooters received minor injuries when Broadsword was strafed. Seaman "Oscar" Whild, who had joined Broadsword for his first experience at sea, was hit by shrapnel, but escaped with torn clothing and a few bruises.

Lt.Cdr. Bray said that, after warning of a raid was given, people continued with their jobs until the very last minute before hitting the deck.

"You could hear your own Bofors booming and the machine-guns chattering," he recalled. "When they stopped, you knew after a few seconds that the ship had been over-flown."

Broadsword was strafed by 30 mm cannon and Lt.Cdr. Bray said: "It makes a pretty sickening noise. You could hear cannon shells thudding into the ship's side."

It was estimated about 40 cannon shells hit the frigate, but they caused remarkably little damage.

Asked what he remembered about the raids, Lt.Cdr. Bray said: "It is like a film you saw three months ago and didn't particularly enjoy. You remember bits of it."

He recalled the quiet in the operations room and the noise elsewhere when the small arms team got going on the upper deck.

"There were lots of bangs and clatters," he said. "If you were under them, you could hear the empty cartridge cases hitting the deck as they fired."

The day after the British landings saw Broadsword and Coventry north-west of the Falklands working together as a missile trap for Argentinian planes. She was back in "bomb alley" on May 23 and outside with Coventry on May 24.

May 25 saw the two warships off Pebble

Heavy weather for HMS Broadsword, but it was preferable to Argentinian bombing raids.

Surrounded by computers and missiles these men and their rifles claimed two aircraft!

Island and Coventry shot down three aircraft with her Sea Dart missiles. Another raid was coming in, but, instead of heading towards Falkland Sound, the planes turned towards Coventry and Broadsword.

"Skyhawks came towards us only 20 to 30 feet above the sea to get under our radar and to make it very difficult to see them against the horizon," said Lt.Cdr. Bray.

The bomb that hit Broadsword struck aft on the starboard side after bouncing off the sea. It struck about halfway between the waterline and the flight deck and tore a gaping hole about 14ft by 8ft in the flight deck.

It tore through a store room and across a passageway and, after blasting through the flight deck, ripped off the front of the Lynx helicopter. Miraculously it failed to detonate.

"It went straight through like a knife through butter," said Lt.Cdr. Bray. "The officer of the watch had seen a bomb hit us, but we did not feel it go through. The initial report was that it had gone straight through the bottom of the ship.

"The next report said it was in the ship and had lodged somewhere. When we learned it had gone straight through, we could not believe our luck."

"We believed we had been leading a charmed life and this confirmed it. Our attention was immediately taken off this problem because the planes had bombed Coventry within about ten minutes. She was hit three times and sank within about twenty minutes."

Broadsword immediately launched all boats, called for helicopters from Falkland Sound, and started to pick up survivors. Some men were in life rafts and some had jumped into the water.

"It was a horrible sight seeing the ship going down," said Lt.Cdr. Bray. "She started to keel over straight away and she had turned upside down and was virtually beneath the waves in about 20 minutes."

Over 170 survivors were taken aboard Broadsword, which then steamed into San Carlos Water to transfer them to a ship leav-

The Argentinian bomb that could have destroyed Broadsword ploughed a trail of destruction before falling harmlessly over the side. It came through the ship's side and up through the flight deck.

go on fighting and we had a better patch put on after the war."

Lt.Cdr. Bray said everyone on board joked about the bomb. "It's amazing how people joke and laugh these things off in those sort of situations," he said.

"There is simply no alternative. One never wants to be seen to be over-concerned about something and the spirit of the ship's company was even higher on bad days than it was on good days."

He summed up the campaign as: "A strange mixture of tragedy, intense excitement and boredom."

Air attacks were not the only problem for the Task Force. Broadsword maintained constant vigilance for possible submarine attack and the ship's electronic eyes and ears had to listen round the clock for any signs of underwater activity.

ing for the carrier group that night. As they left Broadsword in a landing craft, the Coventry survivors raised three cheers in gratitude for their rescue.

Broadsword's engineers found there was no serious damage from the bomb. The flight deck could not be used until repaired, but a second Lynx in the hangar had escaped damage. The after end of the damaged aircraft was later sent home for repairs and further service.

"We were told to go off to the carrier group about 150 miles offshore to lick our wounds," said Lt.Cdr. Bray. "In the next couple of days, we did just that. We managed to weld patches over the holes.

"Our engineers did a marvellous job, working in very cold weather. We were then able to

Lt.Cdr. Bray said he was proud of Broadsword and the achievements of its ship's company, whose average age was about 21.

"I was constantly aware of the close shaves we were having and I will never forget the sinking feeling you get when you hear of people being killed, both Argentinian and British," he said.

"I only ever saw Argentinian planes shot down. It is a horrible thing to see. It is not nice watching a man die like that.

"So you remember that and you remember some of the characters in the ship. You remember some of the people whose sense of humour was superb.

"The spirit on board was incredible. It was like an FA cup final two minutes before the end and you think you are going to win."

The Lynx helicopter only slowed the bomb's progress.

Engineers in the front line

A Royal Engineer's most vivid memory of the battle for the Falklands is being trapped in an Argentinian minefield under fire.

Staff-Sergeant Steve Smith, 29, said it was the most frightening experience of the campaign.

During a night operation, one man suddenly had a foot blown off by a mine in an area where there had been no warning of a minefield. A second man lost a foot when he went to help the casualty.

A helicopter was called in to airlift the casualties and then the Argentinians began shelling the men in the minefield.

"It was June 13 and my wife's birthday. That is why I remember it so well," said Staff-Sgt. Smith, who was serving with 59 Independent Commando Squadron, Royal Engineers.

The squadron, commanded by Major Roddy Macdonald, lost five men in the Falklands and its young sappers, many of them in their teens, were involved in the dangerous business of clearing Argentinian minefields when the fighting was over.

Mines had been sown indiscriminately around Port Stanley by Argentinian army and marine units and no accurate records had been kept. The clearing operation, which 59 Independent Commando Squadron maintained until it sailed for home on June 25, cost three men severe injuries.

The squadron, whose men have all completed arduous commando training and wear the covetted green beret, had 250 officers and men in the Falklands operation.

They included men from 9 Parachute Squadron, Royal Engineers, armoured engineers with combat engineer tractors and two experts from 33 Explosive Ordnance Disposal Regiment.

These two bomb disposal experts tackled an unexploded bomb in the frigate HMS Antelope. The device detonated during their attempts to defuse it and one man was killed and the other severely wounded.

The sappers' motto is "Ubique" and they lived up to it by being everywhere and engaged in a wide variety of tasks during the Falklands campaign.

Lt.Col. Geoffrey Field, commander of Royal Engineers in the Falklands, said: "Sappers were, quite literally, everywhere during the campaign. They were right up the front in every battle clearing mines; some were serving with or took part in special forces operations; they offloaded ships and provided water transport; they dealt with unexploded bombs on ships; they built Harrier strips and bulk fuel systems for the Royal Navy and Royal Air Force; they ran power stations and water treatment plants; they repaired buildings, built bridges and fought as infantry."

Major Macdonald said: "We supported every single phase of the battle. It was an all-embracing task."

He was on board HMS Fearless for the voyage down to the Falklands and was deeply involved in the planning for the landings, working with the staff of 3rd Commando Brigade.

His squadron was split between a number of ships and cross-decking by helicopter was essential during the build-up to the landings. Army sappers from the squadron became used to being winched down from helicopters on to the equipment-packed decks of their ships.

The squadron remained on board ship from early April until the landings on May 21. Members of the squadron landed with the units they were supporting and one troop built an emergency fuel installation for Harriers and helicopters at an existing airstrip at Port San Carlos.

Argentinian air strikes harassed the men at the beach-head and caused a major unloading problem. The logistic landing ship, Sir Lancelot, was hit by two 1,000 lb bombs. Neither exploded, but the squadron office was wrecked and the ship, hit soon after the

When the war was over one of the major problems was locating and clearing mines. The Argentinians had scattered mines from helicopters and had not kept proper records of their locations. Many of these mines were small and made of plastic and thus were extremely difficult to detect. Here sappers of 59 Independent Commando Squadron, Royal Engineers are pictured clearing the minefield at Stanley Airport.

devastating explosion in HMS Antelope, was evacuated.

Leaving Sir Lancelot in a hurry meant some of the squadron lost equipment and Major Macdonald recalled: "It caused a lot of problems. All my stores were in Sir Lancelot. Parties had to go back to grab what stores they could. We had no boats of our own for the operation."

On May 27 the squadron lost Sapper Pradeep Ghandi, 24, who was killed during an air raid. Three others were injured, two badly enough to be evacuated. Corporal Mick Melia, who was married and lived in Plymouth, was killed during 2 Para's attack on Goose Green the next day.

Members of the squadron were involved in a great deal of patrolling to find safe routes forward for the British advance and the patrolling went on until the main attack on June 12.

Major Macdonald said that clearing mines at Darwin and Goose Green had been done by probing for them with a bayonet. Metal detectors had been useless in locating mines made from plastic.

Men from the squadron were deeply involved in supporting 42 Commando in the capture of Mount Harriet and Goat Ridge, 45 Commando at Two Sisters and 3 Para at Mount Longdon. A troop from the squadron was attached to the Welsh Guards and led the battalion to safety when it became trapped in an un-marked minefield.

The Plymouth-based sappers took about one hour to clear routes through the mines for the Guards, working in the dark under shellfire.

When the Argentinian surrender came, men in the squadron's recce troop were the first green beret men to march into Port Stanley with members of 2 Para.

"In Port Stanley, I got hold of the Argentinians' chief engineer, Colonel Durago, and I de-briefed him and grabbed as many Argentinian engineers as I could," said Major Macdonald.

"I knew I had to clear the minefields. I did not expect a problem. We had no problem at Goose Green, where we followed the Argentinian plans and used prisoners to help clear mines."

Major Macdonald said that the fact that there were two sets of plans, one army and one marine, for the minefields around Port Stanley was the first signal that the clearing operation was not going to be straightforward.

It was not long before it became clear the problem of the mines was monumental. There were more mines than shown on plans, and, worse still, mines in areas were none was marked.

Three men from the squadron lost feet during the clearance operations after the surrender. After that, the Plymouth sappers worked to mark the minefields before they sailed for home in Canberra.

In the days after the surrender, members of the squadron built water points, helped repair damaged installations and repaired the Port Stanley runway for the arrival of the first RAF Hercules.

Staff-Sgt Smith paid tribute to the young men in the squadron. "I think our young sappers rose to the occasion," he said. "Everyone knocks the Services of today. But I think their professionalism and fitness is second to none. They earned every last penny of their pay in the Falklands."

He recalled being with the Welsh Guards when they secured the start line for 42 Commando's attack on Mount Harriet. "I have never seen anything so frightening as Harriet being pounded by artillery and naval gunfire before our people went in," said Staff-Sgt Smith.

"I watched the ensuing fire-fight from about 500 metres. It was like an enormous fire-work display."

Staff-Sgt. Trevor Collins, 36, was with 2 Para at Goose Green and recalled: "It was pretty horrific. Our job was to find and deal with minefields, but the action was so fast that we moved up with the fighting troops and we were in the thick of the battle.

"When we came across two minefields, all we could do at that stage was suggest a route through them and mark it."

Staff-Sgt. Collins described the fierce fighting from rise to rise in the terrain as "very frightening" with a lot of very accurate mortar fire from the Argentinians.

"After the battle, we went out with Argentinian prisoners, who had laid the minefields, and they helped us find the mines. They were relieved it was all over. You could tell that. Many of them were very young. They were in pretty poor condition.

"Looking back? It was an experience.

From the engineering point of view it was very good. We had never had the opportunity of working on live minefields before. It was very valuable experience."

Staff-Sgt. Collins said his worst experience was in the closing stage of the campaign in the advance by 2 Para on Wireless Ridge.

"We advanced too fast for the supporting artillery fire and rushed and took the objective," he recalled. "Then we found the supporting artillery fire raining down and a para near me was killed by shrapnel from an air burst.

"It was terrific going into Port Stanley. We knew it was all over. I was very relieved to be in the land of the living. Local people gave us food and tea. It was quite an atmosphere."

Lance-Corporal Barry Heap, 24, recalled being on a reconnaissance patrol with four Welsh Guards near Mount Harriet.

The patrol found itself in a minefield and L/Cpl. Heap neutralised a mine and then brought the patrol safely together before leading them to cover under small arms fire. An enemy patrol passed near them as they lay low and L/Cpl Heap then cleared a way from cover to meet up with another Guards patrol, which had taken four prisoners.

He and another sapper, L/Cpl. Woods, cleared routes to get both patrols and the prisoners into cover and cleared a safe route to lead them to safety before dawn.

"Clearing mines is relatively easy," said L/Cpl. Heap. "Most of the mines were laid on the surface, although some were well hidden in the grass. It is easy enough to neutralise them. It was just a case of remembering your drill and the training you had been given.

"Looking back, I am quite glad of the experience. It was hairy at times, but I would not have missed it.

"When the shells were landing nearby, you just had to hope for the best."

Ready For Anything Royal Fleet Auxiliary

The man who commanded one of the Royal Fleet Auxiliary logistic landing ships in the thick of the action in the battle for the Falklands, was awarded the Distinguished Service Cross in the campaign honours list.

Captain Tony Pitt, 43, commanded Sir Percivale. One of his exploits was to navigate his ship in the dark through eleven miles of confined waters to take vital supplies to troops at Teal Inlet.

He did not know whether the waters had been mined or whether there were enemy troops on the nearby shore.

Sir Percivale was near her sister-ships Sir Bedivere, Sir Galahad and Sir Lancelot when all three were hit by bombs in San Carlos Water. Miraculously all three survived that attack and Sir Percivale came home without a scratch.

So did the helicopter support ship, Engadine, which provided a repair base for the helicopters so crucial to the campaign in terrain where there are no roads.

Chief Officer Christopher Smith, Chief Officer of Engadine, arrived back from the Falklands to learn that he had been awarded the Queen's Gallantry Medal for leading a party of volunteers who saved a blazing, abandoned freighter in the English Channel some months previously.

Engadine and Sir Percivale were just two of the 21 Royal Fleet Auxiliary ships without which there could have been no British Task Force. They fuelled the ships, carried munitions, stores and men and anything else that was asked of them.

They were frequently in the front-line and Sir Galahad and Sir Tristram were devastated in an air attack at Fitzroy. Sir Galahad was later sunk as a war grave and Sir Tristram became an accommodation ship in Port Stanley.

It was fitting that Sir Percivale should have been the first British ship to enter Port Stanley two days after the surrender. Captain Pitt signalled the Commodore Amphibious Warfare that the RFA ensign was flying in Port Stanley.

Back came the signal from Commodore Mike Clapp: "I am delighted that you had the honour to be the first ship into Port Stanley since this affair began and, indeed, to lead the Royal Navy. The role of the logistic landing ships in particular in being at the forefront of operations around the Falkland Islands has been put in its correct perspective."

Sir Percivale was deeply laden with stores, munitions, vehicles, helicopters and about 310 troops when she sailed from Marchwood near Southampton to join the Task Force. Stores were rationalised at Ascension Island and men from the Commando Logistic Regiment joined Sir Percivale for the voyage south.

Men from 40 Commando were aboard Sir Percivale to man machine-guns and a Bofors gun, which had been mounted to give her some protection from air attack.

She was the first logistic landing ship into San Carlos Water on D-Day on May 21. She had first line reserves of stores which had to be put ashore without delay.

Replenishment at sea was an everyday occurrence essential to keep warships topped up with food, fuel and ammunition. Here RFA Stromness (foreground) carries out a jackstay transfer with HMS Intrepid.

Mexeflotes were assembled from sections carried on board. They were powered by outboard engines and ferried guns, vehicles, munitions and rations ashore.

The Argentinian air force directed savage air strikes from early that first day, but they were aimed at the Royal Navy ships providing an air defence umbrella over the landings. The landing ships were unscathed.

Captain Pitt moved to a new anchorage each night so that Argentinian pilots could not predict his position. Sir Percivale was only about one mile from HMS Antelope when she exploded. May 24 saw Sir Percivale only a short distance from her three sistership when they were hit by bombs.

"It was our first chance to use our Bofors gun," said Captain Pitt. "The gunner aimed at an Argentinian Mirage and had it in his sights when there was an electrical fuse fault in the gun system and it would not fire!

"Our machine-guns were firing all the time. My position during air attacks was on the bridge and I could see everything that was going on.

"The amount of lead going up in San Carlos was a great deterrent to the Argentinian pilots and it was very good for our morale. Your only thought was to see the Argentinian aircraft shot down," said Captain Pitt.

Sir Percivale completed unloading and went out during the night of May 24 to join the carrier group to pick up more stores. She was only a couple of miles from the container ship Atlantic Conveyor when it was hit by an Exocet missile.

Captain Pitt took his ship close in on the leeward side of the blazing container ship. A strong wind blew dense smoke over Sir Percivale and her crew could do nothing to help fight the blaze. HMS Alacrity was picking up survivors and Captain Pitt stood by.

First ship in Port Stanley was the RFA Sir Percivale after her many exploits in Falklands waters.

May 29 saw Sir Percivale back in San Carlos with more stores for the land forces. She was also acting as a fuelling point for helicopters and logged her 500th deck landing—a normal year would see about two dozen deck landings.

For 24 hours she gave accommodation to 300 Argentinian prisoners and their guards and then left to make the first supply run to Teal Inlet.

Sir Percivale sailed alone and the trip demanded great navigational skill. Captain Pitt had to feel his way into an entrance only about 200 yards wide, not knowing if it was mined, and then follow a difficult channel for eleven miles. The whole trip was accomplished in the dark.

Captain Pitt said it was his worst moment in the campaign. "If we had gone aground or been blown up by a mine, we could have blocked the entrance for ships coming later. We had to rely on radar to get into the inlet and navigate through it," he said.

The citation for Captain Pitt's DSC refers to that first supply run to Teal Inlet and praises him for "considerable qualities of leadership, co-operation and courage."

It goes on: "Sir Percivale was called to duties far beyond those that would reasonably be expected of her, considering her very light armament and her normal role. It was through Captain Pitt's drive, energy and cheerful enthusiasm that the ship performed all that was asked of her with efficiency and timeliness which were an example to all."

The citation concludes: "Captain Pitt's performance in the face of great danger on many occasions was in the highest traditions of the Royal Fleet Auxiliary Service."

Captain Pitt said: "As far as I am concerned, the medal was for the whole of my ship's company."

Sir Percivale made a number of supply runs to Teal Inlet and was in San Carlos when the surrender was announced.

"It was marvellous," said Captain Pitt. "There was a feeling of jubilation and surprise that it had happened so quickly. Life began returning to normal."

Sir Percivale's siren blared when she became the first British ship into Port Stanley on June 16 and the little community's cathedral answered with its bells. A battle ensign from Sir Percivale was given to hang with other ensigns in the cathedral.

In Port Stanley, Sir Percivale provided three days of rest and recreation to men from 45 Commando after their epic "yomp" across East Falkland and she made two more trips to Teal Inlet before sailing for home.

Seven days after she was hit so tragically at Fitzroy, Sir Galahad still burns. She was later sunk as a war grave.

By the end of the campaign, Sir Percivale had logged her 1,000th helicopter deck landing—a record which cost her captain more celebration drinks.

Captain Pitt said: "I am very pleased we accomplished what we set out to do. My ship's company did a terrific job. It brought everyone together working for the common cause."

Chief Officer Smith said that Engadine sailed from Plymouth with the hastily-formed 847 Squadronn embarked.

The ship, Britain's only purpose-built helicopter support vessel, was delayed with engine trouble off Lisbon and then called into Gibraltar to take on spares to replace those used in the repairs at sea.

She called at Ascension and then sailed alone towards the Falklands, taking the shortest course to reduce her passage time—other ships had kept to the east to stay out of range of Argentinian aircraft.

Engadine was spotted by an Argentinian maritime patrol plane and was prepared to defend herself with no less than 14 machineguns. She altered course during the night and was not attacked.

After a brief spell with the carrier group inside the Total Exclusion Zone, Engadine headed into San Carlos Water to begin repairing battle-damaged helicopters. Specialist repair staff were flown out to join those already on board and 847 Squadron left to set up its base ashore.

Engadine's repair facilities worked round the clock day after day getting damaged helicopters back into fighting trim. In 28 days after her arrival at San Carlos, Engadine logged nearly 1,000 deck landings.

Her teams repaired 66 helicopters of six different types and ten different types landed on her deck, including a captured Argentinian aircraft.

Chief Officer Smith celebrated his 45th birthday in San Carlos a few days after his ship arrived and he said: "It is a birthday I shall remember."

Engadine was not attacked in San Carlos. Argentinian air strikes had died down by the time she arrived and she anchored close to the shore to make it difficult for attacking planes to line up on her.

"Our only damage was our ensign staff, which was shot in half by our own small arms during live-firing practice on the voyage down," said Chief Officer Smith.

Engadine was congratulated by the Commander-in-Chief Fleet and the Task Force Commander for the part she played in the helicopter war. She remained in San Carlos until well after the surrender and then moved around to Port William to continue helicopter repair work.

The voyage to the South Atlantic was Engadine's first trip across the Equator. Her normal role is the operational training of helicopter crews in waters much closer to home.

Chief Officer Smith said the campaign had underlined the value of intensive training. Some lessons had been learned and he had been surprised how effective improvisation could be when it was necessary.

Looking back, he said he remembered the excitement, the lack of sleep and the feeling of pride in his ship.

"I have never seen morale so high in all my years," he said. "Not only in Engadine, but all the ships I visited. I don't think anyone ever thought the outcome would not be as it was."

Plenty of other merchant men were pressed into action.

Right Top

The luxury P & O liner CANBERRA (here returning to Southampton) played a major part in the campaign. Troop Ship, Assault Ship, Hospital & P.O.W. ferry were all roles undertaken—often at very short notice.

Right Bottom

The mighty QE2 rushed troops to South Georgia, and transferred them to other vessels (as pictured) for the final stage of their journey to the Falklands.

The Major General's war

The Royal Marines officer who hit world headlines as commander of the British land forces in the battle for the Falklands, has dubbed the operation the perfect swansong to his career.

Major-General Sir Jeremy Moore, who has now retired, was knighted for his part in the campaign. He said that commanding the land force was "a privilege no one could ask to have bettered as one's swansong in the service."

He was unstinting in his praise for the units, which took part in the operation.

"I think the operation may well turn out to be a little classic," he said. "It is encapsulated in a time frame and situation. It is unique in the distance at which it was conducted."

Gen. Moore went on: "The principle factor on which the success of the operation relied was the tremendous professionalism, drive and dedication of the force I was privileged to command."

He spoke of the quality of the men from the youngest Royal Marine, soldier, sailor or airman, to the commanders and the staff officers.

He had a special word of praise for his staff and for the achievements of the logisticians.

Gen. Moore said that a telephone call at his home at 3 am on April 2 had signalled the beginning of probably the most exciting week in his life.

It was a week of hectic activity as the 3rd Commando Brigade was reinforced in the amphibious role.

"The young men in the brigade had a light in their eyes. Their morale absolutely shone through," said Gen. Moore. "They were so delighted somehow. There was an electric feeling. We had been sent for to do a job. They were on top of the world."

He went on: "It was not just the men in the brigade and the reinforcements coming to join us. It was the whole atmosphere nationally. There was a tremendous 'We will do it' spirit."

On April 8 Gen. Moore was at Bickleigh Barracks to speak to 42 Commando before they left for the Falklands. A bleak wind sliced across the parade ground as Gen. Moore talked to the officers and men in full battle order.

The veteran, who won the Military Cross in Malaya and a bar to the medal in Brunei, told those who had not been in action before: "Think ahead and you will not be caught out and will perform your duty well."

Gen. Moore believes that first week was important because it set the whole tone for the operation and that tone was maintained until he received the Argentinian surrender in Port Stanley on June 14.

He went to Northwood as land deputy to the Commander-in-Chief and later flew out to take command of the land forces.

Gen. Moore believes the Falklands crisis created an operation tailor-made for 3rd Commando Brigade and the amphibious force in general. The amphibious element had been important throughout the operation.

Royal Navy ships had provided vital gun-

fire support to the land operations and the carrier-borne Harriers had been an integral part of the operation.

The brigade's annual winter training in Norway for its NATO role on the northern flank had proved invaluable for the Falklands operation. The marked difference was that the Falklands were cold and wet in contrast to the cold, but generally dry conditions in Norway.

42 Commando and 45 Commando were chosen for operations in the mountains because of their cold weather experience in Norway.

"It would be a mistake to say the weather was no problem," said Gen. Moore. "But we coped with it much better than the opposition."

He said that the cold and wet had combined to make trench foot a problem for some of the troops.

"A major factor never understood by the Argentinians was that the Commando Brigade and the reinforcing Parachute Battalions are very highly trained troops," said Gen. Moore.

"They are not just Regular forces. They belong to organisations which see themselves as elite. They have a very strong esprit and very high standards of training.

"This enabled them to march the whole way across the island. Yomping in a way the Argentinians never really appreciated we could achieve."

The direct approach over very difficult terrain in appalling weather had achieved the vital element of surprise because the Argentinians had failed to read the warning signs properly.

"We produced our major assault against the main enemy positions by coming down out of the mountain tops," said Gen. Moore.

He spoke of the importance of the carefully co-ordinated silent night attack by three major units in the mountains two nights before he accepted the surrender from Brig. Gen. Mario Menendez.

The 3rd Battalion of the Parachute Regi-

Major-General Jeremy Moore, Royal Marines, the overall commander of the land forces.

Every night Major-General Moore reads a few pages of a Bible, which he keeps in his breast pocket. During the conflict he carried it into action.

ment had taken Mount Longdon in the north, 45 Commando took Two Sisters in the centre and 42 Commando was to the south where it took Mount Harriet.

"To any professional soldier, a night attack is difficult," said Gen. Moore. "A silent night attack is more difficult and a three-battalion attack makes it still more difficult. The mountains added yet another factor."

He said the attack had demoralised the enemy. The three units had got quite close to their objectives before the enemy realised what was happening.

"They knew we were operating in the mountains, but they were not aware they had three battalions to face," said Gen. Moore.

The British troops, including men from the SAS, the Special Boat Squadron and the Royal Marines Mountain and Arctic Warfare Cadre, had carried out intensive patrolling before the big attack was made.

"The initiative was with brigade patrols all the time and they dominated the no man's land between British and Argentinian positions, making sure the information flowed our way and not their's," said Gen. Moore.

The patrols gathered vital intelligence about the enemy's dispositions and strengths and mounted small, offensive operations to demoralise Argentinian forces.

Gen. Moore said that some patrols would slip out under cover of darkness and hide literally within feet of enemy positions. They would observe throughout the next day and then slip silently back to our lines with important information.

"The patrolling in the mountains was of a very high standard and a marvellous example of very high grade soldiering," said Gen. Moore.

He praised the gunfire support from Army gunners and said that Naval gunfire had been an important factor in the campaign.

Looking back on the whole operation, he said things had sometimes been close.

"But if you want to achieve an operation, you must push things close to the limits. The other way leads to stagnation and disaster. I think the operation was a very considerable achievement."

Battered but unbeaten

Captain Christopher Layman, who commanded HMS Argonaut.

A young officer, who dived into a flooded magazine to search for an unexploded bomb, was just one of the heroes of the frigate, HMS Argonaut, during the battle for the Falklands.

Shipmates described Sub.Lt. Peter Morgan's dive into the magazine, where there were two bodies and damaged missiles and ammunition, as "very courageous". He was later awarded the DSC.

Argonaut returned home bearing the scars of her near destruction. She was hit by two 1,000 lbs bombs, but, miraculously, neither exploded.

She ran out of control after being hit and came within 200 yards of disaster on a rocky headland in the Falklands.

Lt.Cdr. Mike Chase, Argonaut's First Lieutenant, said: "It was very close. She could have been a complete write-off if she had not turned away from the land."

Young midshipmen and ratings were blooded in battle and poured anti-aircraft fire at attacking Argentinian planes. They had to man their guns to fend off attacks on the days their ship lay stricken. Even self-loading rifles, "modified" to fire automatically, added to the hail of fire sent up by the frigate.

Argonaut was hit on the day HMS Ardent was sunk and she was only a few hundred yards away from Ardent's sister-ship HMS Antelope, when the Type 21 frigate was torn open by a huge explosion as a bomb went up during an attempt to defuse it.

At that stage, Argonaut still had a 1,000 lbs bomb nestling dangerously in her forward magazine. It was too damaged to be defused and it was eventually lowered over the side after a long and difficult operation.

Argonaut, one of the Leander-class modified to carry Exocet missiles, moved into the entrance of San Carlos Water at first light on the first day of the landings. Her Seacat missiles, two 40 mm Bofors guns and machine guns were part of the anti-aircraft defence to prevent Argentinian planes attacking the amphibious force.

Just after first light, an Aeromacchi plane, armed with rockets and guns, flew low around a headland and swooped to attack Argonaut. Three men, two manning machine guns aft in the frigate, were injured in the attack.

Able Seaman Keith Dallaway, a 24-year-old married man, was badly injured and lost an eye. Another machine-gunner, Leading Seaman George Peel, 26, was hurt less seriously, but Master-at-Arms Graham Francis was badly wounded in the chest.

A Wasp helicopter from the Rosyth-based frigate HMS Plymouth flew in during later attacks to take off the injured after they had been tended by Argonaut's doctor and medical team.

When Skyhawk jets roared low across the water to attack, Lt. Malcolm Hardisty was on the gun direction platform above Argonaut's bridge. With him was Petty Officer Hugh Jones.

"One bomb literally bounced over the gun direction platform and would have taken off PO Jones' head, if he had not been bending down at the time," said Lt. Hardisty.

"A second bomb bounced over the foc'sle after striking the water. I saw one plane come in about 15 to 20ft above the water. I was trying to dig a foxhole in the deck. I counted two planes, stayed up to see three more coming and then hit the deck again."

The problem that faced Argonaut and other ships so close in to hilly terrain was that the Argentinian pilots hugged the contours to defeat sophisticated radars and weapons.

"It was back to the naked eyeball," said Lt.Cdr. Chase. "With our Seacat missiles being fired visually by very young people."

It was a surprise attack by no less than six Skyhawks, which had hugged the cover of nearby land, that spelt disaster for Argonaut.

"We were winding up to full speed to help us manoeuvre and we had wheel to starboard," said Lt.Cdr. Chase. "Two bombs came in at an angle on the port bow. One went into the boiler room and the other went into the forward magazine. There was a small explosion and we think two Seacat missile heads partly exploded."

Able Seaman Matthew Stuart, of Bredon, Gloucestershire, who was eighteen years old that day, and Able Seaman Ian Boldy, a married man from Derby, died in the magazine.

The bomb had torn through the side of Argonaut below the waterline. It shot into a diesel fuel tank, smashed its way through bulkheads in the tank and burst through into the magazine. It hit and damaged the side of the ship before falling back to the deck of the magazine.

"There was a lot of smoke and the forward damage control teams did very well to put out the fire that was started," said Lt.Cdr. Chase. "On the bridge, we were turning towards a headland and realised there was no helm and we were running out of power."

"We had been wanting full speed and with the helm stuck over to starboard, we were heading towards land only about 600 yards away," said Lt.Cdr. Andrew Forsyth, the navigating officer.

What he did not know at that stage was that the boiler and engine rooms were full of steam from a bomb-damaged boiler and they had been evacuated. It was impossible for engineers to respond to his request to stop engines and then put them astern.

They had shut down everything they could before evacuating and it was a gradual reduction of steam pressure in the turbines that

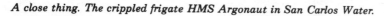

A close thing. The crippled frigate HMS Argonaut in San Carlos Water.

This was one of HMS Argonaut's missile magazines. A bomb ploughed across the ship through fuel tanks smashing through a bulkhead (left) before bouncing off and splitting the ship's side. The unexploded bomb remained for some days in this compartment.

slowed Argonaut down. With her rudder still hard over, the frigate turned away from land.

The anchor was quickly dropped and HMS Plymouth steamed up to offer help and give Argonaut cover.

"Plymouth was always there," said Lt.Cdr. Chase. "She was always in the right place at the right time. She was the quiet heroine of the Falklands. She got on and did everything, and more, that was asked of her."

The bomb aft in Argonaut had wrecked one boiler and she was without her diesel generators—the fuel had been contaminated by sea water.

After dark, Argonaut's sailors struggled to pass a tow, by hand, to HMS Plymouth. It proved impossible for Plymouth to tow the damaged ship and she eventually secured alongside Argonaut to take her into San Carlos Water. Plymouth passed cables to give Argonaut electrical power.

"There was total silence in the ship because of the lack of power," said Lt.Cdr. Chase.

"Ardent was burning in the distance with great bangs and explosions."

Next day, Argonaut got her diesel generators going again and three landing craft were used to move her to another anchorage where she continued to provide air defence as repairs went on.

Army bomb disposal experts defused the 1,000 lbs bomb in the boiler room and it was later lowered over the side. The entry hole just above the water line had already been patched temporarily by a team led by Chief Marine Engineering Mechanic Dave Townsend of Chatham.

He went over the side in a diving suit to position a metal plate over the hole and he worked on in spite of the threat of air attacks.

"I was lowered over the side with a rope round my waist," he said. "Each time there was an air attack they hauled me back on deck.

"I stuck out like a sore thumb in a black suit against the ship's grey side. I would rather have been dropped into the water than remain spreadeagled against her side during an air attack.

"Four times I was pulled up on deck and once I was lowered into the water during air attacks."

The patch took four hours to get into place and CMEM Townsend spent his time half in and half out of the water.

Sub.Lt. Morgan was first to dive to inspect Argonaut's hull outside to ascertain the damage from the bomb forward in the magazine. He found a 2ft hole below the waterline to port and a bulge with a horizontal split below the waterline to starboard.

Other divers from the ship's company positioned a metal plate backed with mattresses over the hole and wedges were used to try to stop the sea water pouring in.

Sub.Lt. Morgan entered the flooded magazine through its one small hatch. There was still a considerable amount of diesel in the compartment, the bodies of the two ratings, the unexploded bomb and damaged missiles and ammunition.

"We had managed to rig up an underwater light, but the visibility was not good," he said. "My job was to locate the bodies, find and assess the condition of the bomb and assess the state of the ammunition and missiles in the magazine.

"I was more conscious of the bodies than the bomb. I found the bodies and I swam almost into the diesel tanks. Then I saw the bomb wedged among Seacat missiles with ammunition boxes on top. I had a hand light and I had a close look at the bomb."

Lt.Cdr. Forsyth said: "It was a very courageous dive. It was a confined space. He did not know what he would find. There was an unexploded bomb among ammunition and no-one knew what condition it was in. He put himself in a great deal of danger."

Sub.Lt. Morgan later dived into the magazine again with a clearance diving officer and plans were made to get the bomb out and put a new patch over the entry hole.

HMS Antelope had anchored not far from Argonaut after being hit and it was while discussions were going on about removing Argonaut's bomb, that Antelope was torn open by her own bomb going off during attempts to defuse it.

Argonaut had enough power to turn her engines and was moved to another anchorage as one of her boats went to help take off Antelope's ship's company.

Air attacks continued in the following days and Argonaut's young sailors spent long hours at action stations.

"We continued fighting the war by day and clearing up and sorting ourselves out by night," said Lt.Cdr. Chase.

Four days after she was hit, Argonaut's ship's company was evacuated, except for a small team led by Captain Christopher Layman, as work began to remove the bomb from the magazine. Decks had to be cut through and debris cleared away. A fire was started and had to be put out and always there was the threat of more air attacks.

Finally the bomb was guided gently up through holes cut in the decks and passed through a "door" cut in the side of the petty officers' mess. It was lowered to the bottom of San Carlos Water.

"It was buoyed because we had not been able to defuse it," said Lt.Cdr. Chase. "It had been too badly damaged to be defused. It could have gone up. It was a great relief to be able to fight the ship without a bomb on board."

Diesel fuel had been spattered on Argonaut's upper works during the bomb attack and unknown wits in the ship's company had daubed defiant graffiti, including "Titanic was never like this" and "Ban the bomb".

When Argonaut sailed from San Carlos the patch forward came off and compartments once again flooded. Further repairs were carried out with assistance from Stena Seaspread before she sailed for home.

During her days in the thick of the action, Argonaut had used 8,000 rounds of machine gun ammunition, 70 rounds of Bofors ammunition and ten Seacat missiles. She shot down one plane and hit at least two more.

"The voyage home was a time for winding down,' said Lt.Cdr. Chase. "We steamed on one boiler with both main engines. We got back to Devonport on June 26.

"Our home-coming was overwhelming. One was totally unable to cope with such a welcome. Everyone coming back said that.

"There was a sense of relief that we had got back safely. A sense of pride that the job was so well done. A sense of pride in the ship's company, who all did particularly well."

HMS PLYMOUTH. ANOTHER LUCKY SURVIVOR...

HMS Plymouth in San Carlos Water after being attacked by the Argentine Air Force in the Falkland Sound. Below decks a major fire was raging.

Damage from a 30mm cannon shell.

OTHER SHIPS WERE NOT SO LUCKY . . .

HMS Coventry—as the bombs exploded . . . By this stage of the war ships were not able to tell stories of lucky escapes from unexploded bombs.

Farewell to a fine ship. Very soon HMS Coventry was to roll over and sink just to the north of West Falkland.

ABANDON SHIP . . .

The crippled frigate HMS ARDENT is doomed—and men jump for their lives . . . HMS YARMOUTH takes all the survivors to safety.

Straight from the shoulder

A Royal Marine missile operator, who destroyed an Argentinian jet during the battle for Goose Green, was so elated the rest of his team had to pull him to the ground.

Marine Rick Strange was Mentioned in Despatches for shooting down an Aeromacchi with a Blowpipe missile. He was under fire as he stood on the battlefield engaging the aircraft with the shoulder-launched weapon.

"I was on such a high after shooting down the aircraft that I didn't sleep for about two nights. I was walking around about 6ft off the deck," said Rick.

He was among the 50 Royal Marines in the Plymouth-based Air Defence Troop sent to the Falklands to use their Blowpipe missiles against enemy planes. The troop was credited with four "kills".

Short Brothers Ltd., of Belfast, who make the Blowpipe system, presented the Air Defence Troop with a large silver figurine to mark the achievement. There were individual statuettes of a Blowpipe missile operator for the men, who shot down planes.

The operators need courage to stand upright to engage an aircraft. The Blowpipe is designed for defence against low level ground attack by aircraft or helicopter gunships and the missile is guided on to its target with a miniature thumb-controlled joystick.

Members of the Air Defence Troop complete a rigorous training at the Royal School of Artillery at Larkhill and must achieve a high degree of success during 1,300 carefully recorded firings on a simulator. Each man fires two live missiles during training and a further one each year after that.

The men must become expert at aircraft recognition and they need quick reactions to spot, identify and engage a plane coming in low and very fast. They are likely to have only a few seconds to make a successful attack.

Colour-Sergeant Mick Tillbrook, 34, was the Air Defence Troop's sergeant-major and he explained that the Falklands terrain and the movement of equipment across it were the biggest problems.

"Blowpipe is such a bulky piece of equipment," he said. "It is not meant to be man-packed for any great distance."

He described the terrain in the Falklands as a mixture of the tors of Dartmoor and the scree slopes of the Lake District. Some members of his troop made the long "yomp" from San Carlos to Port Stanley and they carried Blowpipe equipment much of the time, in addition to their personal weapons and equipment.

At Ascension Island on the way south, the troop got in live firing practice and worked hard with their simulators. They were put ashore early on D-Day at San Carlos to provide air defence before the Rapier missiles could be flown ashore and set up.

Marine Strange, 26, was one of the members of the Air Defence Troop supporting 2 Para in the bitter fighting for Goose Green.

"It was just like a war film, but being in it," he recalled.

The Paras had "rolled up" the Argentinians on a ridge overlooking Goose Green and his team moved forward into an ambush posi-

"Never designed to be manhandled"—these Blowpipe launchers and missiles were carried by the Commandos on their epic "Yomp" across the Falklands.

tion. The Paras advanced over open ground and came under heavy fire from anti-aircraft weapons depressed to fire at them.

The Air Defence Troop men were under mortar fire and Para wounded were falling only a short distance from them. Two Aeromacchi jets came in low to attack and one dropped napalm on Para positions. Marine Strange shot down the second plane.

"I was under fire throughout the attack on the aircraft," he said. "I was just doing a job. There was mortar, small arms and artillery fire. The lot. I saw the aircraft go about 200 metres in a great big ball of flame and then it hit the deck.

"I felt elation. I was jumping up and down with elation. Then I was pulled down to the deck."

He said he reckoned he had hit the plane at the join of the wing and the cockpit.

"I was just engaging a lump of machinery that might have killed me," said Rick.

He said he was surprised how quickly the day of fighting had passed. He had very clear memories of the Argentinian shelling as the Paras advanced on Goose Green.

Marine Wally Walton, 26, is credited with destroying a Mirage jet at Ajax Bay. He fired four missiles in about ten minutes and made his "kill" with the fourth.

One shot detonated prematurely with another missile, one struck the ground and another was fired at a plane crossing his front. He believed it had made the Argentinian pilot veer off course.

"A Mirage came in low and straight at me," he said. "I fired and gathered the missile on target. It was a case of seeing the plane and firing at almost the same time."

The aircraft was seen disappearing trailing smoke and Marine Walton was later credited with its destruction.

"I was quite excited really," he said. "I just wanted to get the plane. It disappeared from my sight trailing smoke. I was busy reloading by then."

Marine Alan Steven, 28, also shot down a Mirage at Ajax Bay.

It was one of three Mirages which swooped over a hill and were immediately engaged by Rapier missiles and anti-aircraft guns. Marine Steven was unable to engage them with Rapier already in operation, but, when a Rapier missed, he fired and hit the middle plane in the tail fin.

"The plane turned over and splashed into the bay," he said. "The pilot tried to eject, but, because the plane was upside down, he hit the cliffs by Port San Carlos.

"I felt pretty good. It proved the thing worked. It was all over in a few seconds."

Marine Steven joined 45 Commando for the march from Ajax Bay to Port Stanley.

"The walk was pretty hard," he said. "The terrain was very much like Dartmoor and it was very wet. Our feet were pretty bad.

"My most vivid memories are shooting the plane down and 45 Commando's attack on Two Sisters."

The men from the Air Defence Troop were close to the action and came under heavy fire. Marine Steven said he watched 45 Commando got in to attack and was surprised they did not have more casualties in the heavy fire brought to bear on them.

"The Argentinians had .5 inch machine-guns," he said. "It was pretty horrendous to watch. The only thoughts we had were that 45 Commando was taking a hell of a battering, but it turned out the other way. Everyone was using tracer. We could see a hell of a lot of that."

Later he and his companions took up positions on Two Sisters to give air defence cover. They could see Port Stanley in the distance.

"When I heard about the surrender, I could not believe it. I thought someone was having me on," said Marine Steven.

Corporal Derek Obbard, 28, is credited with shooting down a Skyhawk at Ajax Bay the day after the British landings.

"Four Skyhawks came up San Carlos Water, very low and very fast," he said. "They were at eye level and I was not very high up. They were not far off the water.

"I engaged the leading aircraft, but I did not see the missile hit because a rogue Rapier missile landed about 10 metres in front of me and exploded.

"Through the sight of my Blowpipe, I saw a cloud of debris coming up just in front of me and I got down. I found out later that the explosion was a rogue Rapier missile. It made a hell of a crater.

"I started the engagement and the missile was going towards the target. Then I went down because of the Rapier explosion. I heard later the plane had gone down and that I was credited with it."

Corporal Obbard "yomped" across to Port

Stanley with 45 Commando and said: "It was hard work, but it's our job. We are fit enough to do it and it was a case of having to."

He has vivid memories of the night attack on Two Sisters and he recalled: "It was amazing seeing tracer going up and down, backwards and forwards.

"I thought at first that 45 Commando was taking a hammering. Then we heard reports of a couple of casualties and it was amazing in view of the fire they were taking from the Argentinians.

"We were under fire a couple of times during the night. We had a few fairly close, but nothing too close. It was a bit hairy at first, but after a while I suppose you got used to it."

Corporal Obbard and his companions set up air defence positions at first light and he recalled gear, ammunition and weapons strewn by the fleeing Argentinians.

"There were rations half-cooked in mess tins. They had definitely been caught by surprise," he said.

Looking back on the long march to Port Stanley, he remembered a few times when they were waiting for equipment to catch up with them and they had to lie on the bare ground and try to sleep. "We were wet most of the time," he said.

"It was magic to hear of the surrender. It was sheer relief that we had come through it and that we would soon be going home. Going into Port Stanley and knowing it was finished is the thing that sticks in my mind. I remember, too, going through the minefields on the way into Stanley and wondering if you would get it after it was all over."

Fly, fly, and fly again

Lieutenant Commander Hugh Clark awarded the Distinguished Service Cross was Commanding Officer of 825 Squadron during the Falklands Operation.

Sea King helicopters from Royal Naval Air Station at Culdrose in Cornwall played a vital part in the rescue of Welsh Guards and crewmen, many severely injured, when the logistic landing ship, Sir Galahad, was hit by bombs at Fitzroy.

Television film of the dramatic rescue was seen all over the world and it showed the great daring of the helicopter crews, who flew dangerously close to the blazing ship, which could have exploded at any time.

The helicopters, three of them from a specially-formed 825 Squadron from Culdrose, saved many lives that day and, after the last man had been brought safely ashore, they ferried the injured to the field hospital at Ajax Bay.

Lt.Cdr. Hugh Clark, who commanded 825 Squadron, said: "It was bloody awful. There were dozens of injured. It is the nastiest memory of the campaign for me."

He had flown a surveying party into Fitzroy settlement shortly before the Argentinian air attack on Sir Galahad and Sir Tristram.

"We heard jets coming and we knew they were not friendly," he said. "We heard the first bombs start to fall and we took cover. Then the planes were through and out again. I crawled out from under a bulldozer and ran about 100 yards to my aircraft.

"I jumped in and flashed it up. The ships were already burning. It was quite obvious we were going to have to save some lives. We got airborne. A couple of other helicopters had arrived."

Lt.Cdr. Clark, who was awarded the Distin-guished Service Cross in the campaign Honours List, said that, at one time or another, five Sea Kings and a Wessex helicopter were involved in the rescue.

Sea Kings from 825 Squadron, captained by Lt. Phil Sheldon and Lt. John Boughton, plucked to safety troops and crew mustered in an extremely confined area of Galahad's foredeck. Many of the survivors were injured or in shock.

The pilots flew dangerously close to the mast and rigging of the stricken ship. There was little clearance and ammunition and other stores in Galahad were constantly ex-ploding. Both Lt. Sheldon and Lt. Boughton were awarded the Queen's Gallantry Medal.

Lt.Cdr. Clark said: "It was quite obvious to me there were enough helicopters forward on the Galahad. I decided to look around to find people not being looked after. There were those trapped aft or who had already jumped off the ship and were being swept towards the after end by wind and current.

"We picked up about twelve in my heli-copter. We picked them up in penny numbers and took them straight to the beach. The fly-ing was not particularly difficult in spite of the smoke.

"We went at it in a calculated fashion," said Lt.Cdr. Clark. "We took it slowly. It was all done in reasonable time and we picked up all the men in the water. Some were in a dreadful state."

Liferafts full of survivors, some badly in-jured, remained dangerously close to the blazing ship. Helicopter crews took off injured men and then blew the liferafts away from the ship with the down-draught from their rotors.

"I suppose the rescue went on for a couple of hours," said Lt.Cdr. Clark. "I lost track of time. After the injured had been given first aid on shore, we had to fly them to the Ajax Bay hospital. We flew until after dark doing this."

His squadron, formed from scratch in only a few days at Culdrose, near Helston, was one of four from the air station to take part in operations in the South Atlantic.

At the height of the crisis, Culdrose had over 1,000 men with 50 Sea King helicopters involved in the campaign. Staff at Culdrose were involved in a large-scale back-up operation to maintain a supply of engines, spares and stores. Support was also provided for the families of the men away with the Task Force.

Lt.Cdr. Ralph Wykes-Sneyd, who was awarded the Air Force Cross, commanded 820 Squadron embarked in HMS Invincible. One of the squadron pilots was Prince Andrew, who flew exactly the same sorties as the rest of the squadron.

820 Squadron's primary task was to protect the Task Force from submarine attack and during the conflict its pilots flew for 64 days out of 66 on a continuous 24-hour basis. Much of the flying was in poor weather or fog, but the squadron maintained its surveillance for Argentinian submarines, which could have spelt disaster to the British ships.

Sea Kings from Culdrose in 826 Squadron, commanded by Lt.Cdr. Doug Squier, were embarked in HMS Hermes and their job, too, was to maintain constant vigilance for enemy submarines. Lt.Cdr. Squier was awarded the Air Force Cross and he was said to have "held his squadron together and maintained their exceptionally high morale to do what must be recorded as one of the longest sustained periods of continuous intensive flying in the his-

tory of British aviation, meeting every task however difficult or dangerous with determination and enthusiasm."

Typical of the spirit of 826 Squadron was the night of the SAS raid on Pebble Island when atrocious weather conditions and winds of up to 75 knots forced the escort to sail, leaving Hermes to proceed alone.

Although the conditions were way outside the limits of helicopter operations, 826 Squadron flew to provide anti-submarine defence and surface warning for the carrier so that operations could continue.

826 Squadron lost two aircraft because of the intense pressures of operational flying, but both aircrews were rescued from their ditched Sea Kings.

Culdrose also had 824 Squadron subdivided into flights on board a number of Royal Fleet Auxiliaries to fly in the anti-submarine role.

Lt.Cdr. Ian McKenzie, who was awarded the MBE for his contribution during the conflict, was ordered to disembark his flight on

Lt. Phil Sheldon (left) and Lt. John Boughton who both won the Queen's Gallantry Medal for their Fitzroy rescue missions.

June 3 to operate ashore at the San Carlos bridgehead.

With little time for preparation and with minimal commando flying training, his three aircraft flew almost continuously for four days unloading essential stores, ammunition and equipment from ships in San Carlos Water.

Lt.Cdr. Clark's hastily formed 825 Squadron also had little experience in military operations beyond the anti-sub-

Home sweet home Falklands style. Off duty naval airmen relax in makeshift accommodation.

marine role. But the squadron quickly adapted to operations ashore in the Falklands and played a crucial part in the advance and final operations before the surrender.

When the conflict erupted, Lt.Cdr. Clark was commanding 706 Squadron at Culdrose, dealing with advanced flying training and operational flying training.

Clearly training must continue during the South Atlantic campaign, but Service chiefs quickly recognised the need for more heavy lift helicopters—the Sea King can lift three tons underslung.

Lt.Cdr. Clark, who returned to Culdrose to command 706 Squadron, was simply told to form a new squadron.

"I was given carte blanche as far as the people I wanted in the squadron," he said. "I was asked what manpower, equipment and back-up I needed for a squadron of ten Sea Kings. I selected my key people, the second-in-command, the senior pilot and the air engineer officer and gave them their tasks."

He started to form the squadron on May 3 and it was commissioned on May 7. A few days later, the ten helicopters, 36 aircrew, 100 maintainers and their stores were heading south.

"You have to understand the concept of the Falklands spirit," said Lt.Cdr. Clark. "I could say what I wanted and I got it."

In just a few days, the Sea Kings for the squadron had their anti-submarine sonars removed, extra radios for communications with Army units fitted and their white markings painted out with black to make them less obvious as a target.

The men were rapidly equipped with unfamiliar camouflaged clothing and Arctic survival equipment. Lt.Cdr. Clark obtained a rifle for each man, a pistol for all "front-seat" aircrew and a sub-machine gun for "back-seat" aircrew.

Two helicopters and some of the squadron,

including the command team, sailed in the QE2. The other eight aircraft and the majority of the men sailed south in the Atlantic Causeway from Devonport. About 30 men went to the Falklands in the helicopter support ship, Engadine, and arrived well after the main body of the new squadron.

The squadron was tasked to support 5 Infantry Brigade, but, in the event, it found itself supporting any of the units ashore as the advance on Port Stanley developed.

Atlantic Causeway made the fastest passage in the Task Force and was disembarking 825 Squadron's helicopters at San Carlos on May 28. The other aircraft transferred from QE2 to Canberra at South Georgia, after providing essential heavy-lift cross-decking between QE2, Canberra and Norland in Grytviken.

The squadron got together in a field at Port San Carlos at the beginning of June and moved next day to San Carlos Settlement, where it remained for the rest of the campaign.

"We lived at first in tents we had begged, borrowed or stolen from other people," said

It was never like this at Culdrose! Local "residents" cross the main runway ashore in the Falklands.

Lt.Cdr. Clark. "We had a primitive field kitchen and no other facilities. We used the beach as heads.

"We lived there for seven or eight days in wind, rain and sleet. We were subject to air raid warnings at all hours of the day and night and had to retire to our trenches."

Gradually, as the Army moved out, the squadron was able to move into proper accommodation, with aircrew first to move into the settlement manager's house to ensure them adequate sleep in comfort. They were flying dawn to dusk every day, sometimes under fire.

Lt.Cdr Clark found that his maintenance teams were under-employed.

"We used to take off at dawn, go away to do our jobs and come back at dusk," he said. "There was no planned maintenance. We let the aircraft run. We did only wartime contingency servicing, which virtually meant topping up the oil. We only replaced something when it broke."

The squadron had few problems with the weather and flew in a wide variety of roles. Aircrews stoked up with a big breakfast before take off and then snatched what snacks they could during the day.

"We did not stop," said Lt.Cdr. Clark. "We kept flying until we came back at last light. We refuelled wherever we could. Fuelling was always a problem. You had to think about it all the time. You had to have enough gas to get home.

"If you stopped, you would keep the motor going. You would spend 9 to 9½ hours strapped to your seat. We ate biscuits and

chocolate at half time. Lots of the ships would come up with soup when we landed. Sometimes we got a fish and chip supper, which we ate in the cockpit."

Lt.Cdr. Clark went on: "At dusk, we came back and parked for the night. During the fighting, we dispersed the aircraft and you

Prince Andrew saw his share of South Atlantic action.

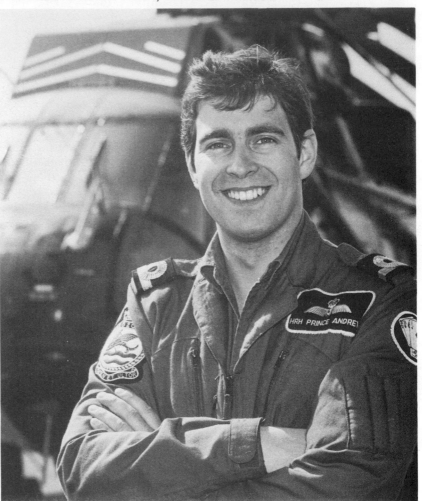

had to hike back after parking and hike to get your aircraft next morning. We had our second big meal at supper and then relaxed, perhaps to write a letter, before going to bed."

The squadron found itself involved in every sort of operation in support of the push towards Port Stanley.

"We did absolutely everything," said Lt.Cdr. Clark. "Troop and artillery movements, food supply, ammunition supply,

One of many happy home-comings. Lt.Cdr. Ian McKenzie meets baby Alexander for the first time. His wife, Sue, and sons Douglas and Jamie complete the welcome.

Upperdeck cargo . . . The Flight Deck of HMS Hermes—Bombs and Missiles ready for the Sea Harrier raids against shore targets on 1st May 1982.

flying in surveying parties, movement between ships and San Carlos, carrying the Press and casualty evacuation.

"Normally, we would carry 16 fully-equipped soldiers. But we had up to 20 SAS with all their guns and funny stuff. They would literally strap-hang.

"We flew the aircraft to their limits. If it seemed to be working okay, we would accept it."

Several of the squadron's aircraft were hit by bullets or shrapnel and some came under artillery and mortar fire when ferrying troops to the front.

825 Squadron was kept busy after the surrender until it began the journey home on July 15. It was disbanded at Culdrose on September 16.

Lt.Cdr. Clark said: "Looking back, I believe it was the right thing to do. What reinforced my belief in the rightness of it was when we started to meet the islanders and their children.

"When we were involved in liberating little settlements, we saw the joy of liberated people and the misery of the Argentinians. They were kids. A lot of them were conscripts from the January intake.

"And the response of our men under pressure when they realised what had to be done never ceases to amaze me. They just got on with it."

Unsung heroes

Lt.Col. Ivar Hellberg who commanded the Commando Logistic Regiment.

Unsung heroes of the Falklands campaign were the men of Commando Logistic Regiment, Royal Marines, who kept the whole of the British land force re-supplied with ammunition, food and other vital stores under the most difficult conditions.

There can never have been a longer supply line than the 8,000 miles from Britain to the Falkland Islands and it meant the "Loggies" had to get their sums right before they even sailed for the South Atlantic.

Once in the Falklands, where there are virtually no roads, they faced the problem of moving almost all their stores forward by helicopter.

In simple terms, the regiment was responsible for making sure the front-line units in 3rd Commando Brigade and, later, in 5 Infantry Brigade, were kept supplied during the advance and attacks in some of the most inhospitable terrain in the world.

The work of the Commando Logistic Regiment's Medical Squadron at the improvised hospital at Ajax Bay was much publicised during the campaign. There was little recognition for the rest of the regiment, whose contribution was vital to the British victory.

"Loggies" in the Base Support Area at Ajax Bay worked long hours making sure rations and war stores went forward. They lived in improvised shelters, often soaking wet and were subjected to frequent enemy air strikes. Their saddest task was to bury the dead.

Seven men were killed and 37 wounded in Argentinian air attacks on the Base Support Area—Royal Marines Lance-Corporal Colin Davison was killed by enemy cannon fire while firing his machine-gun at a Skyhawk at point-blank range.

The Commando Logistic Regiment was commanded by Lt.Col. Ivar Hellberg, of the Royal Corps of Transport. About 80 per cent of the regiment were Royal Marines, about 15 per cent were from Army units and the rest were from the Royal Navy, most of them with the Medical Squadron.

The Army and Royal Navy men are all commando-trained, wearing their own cap badges on the covetted green beret. The whole regiment is trained to fight in the rifle role, if the need arises.

The Falklands campaign started for the "Loggies" on April 2, the day the regiment was scheduled to begin Easter leave. By 7am that day, the whole unit was back in camp beginning the intense preparations for the long voyage south.

"The problem with outloading the entire war stocks of a brigade at short notice should never be under-estimated," said Lt.Col. Hellberg, who added: "I was pleasantly surprised, in spite of a number of snags, that the regiment was loaded and ready to go some 36 hours after the alert had been given."

Under his command in the Falklands, Lt.Col. Hellberg had about 850 officers and men. Units attached to his regiment included a Rapier battery, a Blowpipe anti-aircraft unit, an amphibious beach unit, a

HQ for the Commando Logistic Regiment. This old refrigeration plant at Ajax Bay was soon bustling with activity. A helicopter landing pad, ammunition dump, hospital and base support facilities were created. Improvisation was the order of the day.

satellite communications team, Royal Navy and RAF bomb disposal teams, a field records office and the postal organisation.

"We were desperately short of helicopters," said Lt.Col. Hellberg. "The problem was compounded by the loss of the Atlantic Conveyor, which was bringing me more helicopters. Her loss badly affected my ability to get things forward and it delayed the push forward for some time.

"Helicopters were absolutely critical. We did not have enough and you could not risk helicopters by day when air attacks were threatened."

In round terms, the regiment took 17,000 tons of stores out from England, including 8,600 tons of ammunition. In the Falklands, some 9,080 tons of stores were sent forward. They included 3,500 tons of ammunition, 1,200 tons of rations, 300 tons of hexamine fuel, 90 tons of biscuits, 1,400 tons of fuel and 280 tons of defence stores.

While the remainder of the regiment coped with a number of changes in plans

immediately after the landings, the Medical Squadron, led by Surgeon-Commander Rick Jolly, was making the best of things in a long-abandoned refrigeration plant.

At Ajax Bay, Surg.Cdr. Jolly had just under 100 staff including men from the squadron, from a Royal Army Medical Corps unit at Aldershot and a 22-strong surgical support team from the Royal Navy Hospital, Plymouth, led by Surg.Lt.Cdr. Philip Shouler.

They set up their hospital in a plant once used for freezing sheep carcases.

"It was filthy and dusty, but dry," said Surg.Cdr. Jolly. "The walls were made of cork insulating material and, although it took a while to warm up, it stayed warm.

"We had just under 24 hours before we received our first casualties."

That time was used to clear up as much as possible, to set up a basic organisation and to prepare two rooms as operating theatres. By the end of the campaign, the hospital had dealt with 650 battle casualties, including

150 from Sir Galahad, and another 300 with problems such as trench foot and exposure.

It was only six days after landing that the regiment received its most severe air attack when 12 x 400 kilogram bombs were dropped on the base support area at Ajax Bay. Only four exploded.

"One of the bombs exploded in the area of the regimental galley and the echelon of 45 Commando, killing six men and seriously wounding 26 others. If this had happened half an hour earlier, the galley would have been full and there would have been far more casualties," said Lt.Col. Hellberg.

Another bomb exploded among ammunition and the ammunition went on exploding throughout the night. Three unexploded bombs hit the Medical Squadron's makeshift hospital, one going straight through and two lodging in the building where they became an accepted part of life to the "medics".

"Despite the appalling carnage, shock and sorrow, the men got straight on with rescuing the wounded away from the exploding ammunition and attempting to put out the fires," said Lt.Col. Hellberg.

The unexploded bombs in the hospital building meant the Medical Squadron had to shrink into 50 per cent of the space it had originally occupied. The life-saving work went on, even during air raids, with battle-injured casualties being prepared for the flight by helicopter to the hospital ship, Uganda.

Originally, Uganda stayed about 30 miles off Falkland Sound in the so-called Red Cross box, but later she moved each day to within ten minutes flying time from Ajax Bay to take off the casualties.

After treatment in Uganda, the casualties were usually taken to Montevideo by Royal Navy survey ships in a new role as "ambulance" ships and then flown home by RAF VC 10 aircraft.

Surg.Cdr. Jolly described the facilities for the casualties as a tri-Service medical triumph.

He said that the sense of humour and dedication shown by characters in the television series "MASH" was very much borne out in the hospital at Ajax Bay, despite the horrible wounds being dealt with and the physical dangers of bombing in the constant air raid alerts.

Whistles were used to warn of air raids and

Surg.Cdr. Jolly said: "I still cannot pass a football field and hear the referee's whistle without feeling a tightening in my gut."

Resuscitation, life-saving and limb-saving surgery were the priorities at the Ajax Bay hospital. Surg.Cdr. Jolly described it as battle surgery. Dead and infected tissue was removed from wounds and shattered limbs were immobilised ready for the patient's transfer to Uganda.

British casualties were first treated in the field by other soldiers and Royal Marines in the buddy-buddy system and then flown back, often under fire, in helicopters of 3rd Commando Brigade Air Squadron.

Surg.Cdr. Jolly said it was often the sheer fitness of the young casualties which enabled them to hang on to life in spite of appalling injuries.

"We worked as long as the injured were coming in," he said. "Into the early hours of the morning sometimes. During the 14 hours of night there was usually nothing to do but clean up, make ready and get your head down before the next lot came in."

Regulations allow a tot of spirits to be issued in exceptional conditions and Surg.Cdr. Jolly issued a tot to his staff on 11 occasions during the hardest days and nights at Ajax Bay.

He said the "medics" in red, green or blue berets had the satisfaction of feeling their duty had been done. Every British casualty admitted alive at Ajax Bay had gone out alive. Only two Argentinian casualties had died and they had been admitted some time after sustaining extremely serious injuries.

Lt.Col. Hellberg had this tribute for the Ajax Bay "medics": "They were fantastic. They worked round the clock and during air raids."

He said that after the Fitzroy attacks on Sir Galahad and Sir Tristram, the Ajax Bay hospital was inundated with injured, many with severe burns.

"Virtually all the men were involved with the wounded at this time—often simply by sitting beside the stretchers comforting those in fearful pain. The men were magnificent," said Lt.Col. Hellberg.

He talked of the magnitude of the logistics problem of keeping the land forces supplied as they moved east towards Port Stanley and the final Argentinian white flag.

The "Loggies" ferry ashore heavy equipment and portable roads, neatly rolled ready to be laid, from a landing craft at San Carlos.

Every man in the two brigades had to carry two days supply of food and ammunition, all vehicle fuel tanks had to be full and each gun and mortar had to have 500 rounds at hand before the major assaults, with another 500 rounds available in re-supply.

After the surrender had been received by Major-General Jeremy Moore, the Commando Logistic Regiment had to move from Ajax Bay to Port Stanley as soon as possible to support the force concentrated in that area.

A party was left behind at Ajax Bay to look after 40 Commando and other units in the area and a large guarding party remained to look after 500 special category Argentinian prisoners, mostly officers. At Port Stanley, the regiment spent a lot of time helping to clear up the mess left by the defeated Argentinians.

Lt.Col. Hellberg paid tribute to the Anglo-Saxon ability to find a way around problems and he stressed the value of humour, without which life would have been miserable.

"It was a hell of an experience," he said. "It was a great privilege to have gone through it. You know how good your training is and you know the limitations of your training.

"The men were fantastic. There is no doubt the Royal Marines and Paras won the war and there is no doubt my men won the logistic battle through their enormous determination and industry."

Battle zone surgery

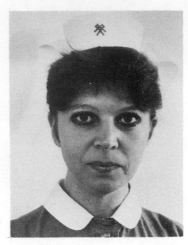

Senior Naval Nurse June Hendy, one of the girls who sailed south with the Task Force.

An over-riding memory for many staff from Plymouth's Royal Naval Hospital, who sailed to the South Atlantic with the Falklands Task Force, is of the great courage shown by the wounded.

That courage is typified by the young man brought from the battlefield to the hospital ship, Uganda, whose leg had to be amputated without general anaesthetic.

Senior Naval Nurse June Hendy, 26, one of seven women nurses and six women nursing officers from the Royal Naval Hospital to sail to the South Atlantic, sat and held the man's hand during the operation.

The man's medical history dictated that doctors could not give him a general anaesthetic and he was given anaesthetics which numbed the lower part of his body. He was screened from the procedure, but he was fully conscious throughout.

"I held his hand and talked to him," recalled Senior Naval Nurse Hendy. "The operation took about an hour. I suppose he was about 25 years old. He was married and I remember talking to him about his wife. He was very brave and he had a sense of humour.

"We had another lad, who had severe stomach injuries and had lost an arm. He had to keep coming back to the operating theatre and he was super. He had to have dressings changed and he was very brave. They were all very brave."

Bravery was often seen by staff from the Royal Naval Hospital, who found themselves whisked from the ordered routine of hospital life in Plymouth 8,000 miles to a battle zone.

The hospital sent 12 doctors, a dentist, 13 women nurses and nursing officers and 41 medically trained ratings with a wide variety of specialisations.

A complete surgical support team of 24 spent its war ashore at Ajax Bay dealing with battle casualties in an abandoned freezer plant, which was turned into a makeshift hospital by Commando Logistic Regiment's Medical Squadron.

Doctors, nurses and medical assistants from the Royal Naval Hospital served in Uganda and Canberra and some doctors and ratings were sent to serve in warships needing medical staff for the conflict.

Women staff forsook their crisp uniforms for their role at sea and instead adopted the shirts, trousers and the ubiquitous "woolly pulleys" worn by the men of all the Services.

"When the wounded lads came on board, they came from awful situations," said Senior Naval Nurse Hendy. "When they saw a female face, I think they felt safe because women were there.

"I think it was nice for them to see a woman. The nurses made an effort to look nice for them. Because we wore shirts, pullovers and trousers, you had to do something with the top to try to look attractive."

Senior Naval Nurse Hendy, a naval nurse for six years, worked in the operating theatre on Uganda and casualties airlifted to the ship by helicopter were often brought to the theatre still in combat gear.

"The anaesthetist would explain what was going to happen," said Senior Naval Nurse

Hendy. "He would then pop them off to sleep and we would put the patient in the right position for surgery.

"We also had a lot of patients coming back into the theatre for routine treatment. Obviously, it was hard work. It was upsetting because the injuries like burns were disfiguring.

"Men, who had amputations, would wake up and ask you if their leg was still there, or how much had been taken off. Sometimes you felt very choked up inside. But the patients were tremendous. Their morale was so good. Each patient seemed to help the others."

Senior Naval Nurse Hendy added: "I would not have liked to have been left behind. Nursing-wise, it was good experience. But I would not like to have to go again for a long time."

Naval Nurse Geraldine Hodgson, 23, was also in Uganda and she remembers the high morale of the wounded and their willingness to try to help the nursing staff.

"For someone, who had not been qualified a year at that stage, it was an experience I will never forget in my whole life," said Naval Nurse Hodgson.

Senior Nursing Officer Jean Kidd, who is in charge of the casualty department at the Royal Naval Hospital, ran the casualty reception area on Uganda.

"Our job was to assess, sort and resuscitate," she said. "It was very noisy. The flight deck was just above us. The area we used had been a children's play area."

In one exceptional day, 160 casualties flooded aboard Uganda, but usually the staff could expect between 40 and 70 wounded when the fighting was at its height.

"Initially, it was quite overwhelming," said Senior Nursing Officer Kidd. "But there was so much going on there was no time to think.

"You realised how important families and friends were to the men. And how many wanted to see their mothers. I think they were very surprised to see women on the ship.

"Men like women to talk to when they are ill. They like a nice soft hand to hold. It is

The hospital ship Uganda. Many men owe their lives to the skill of her surgeons and nurses.

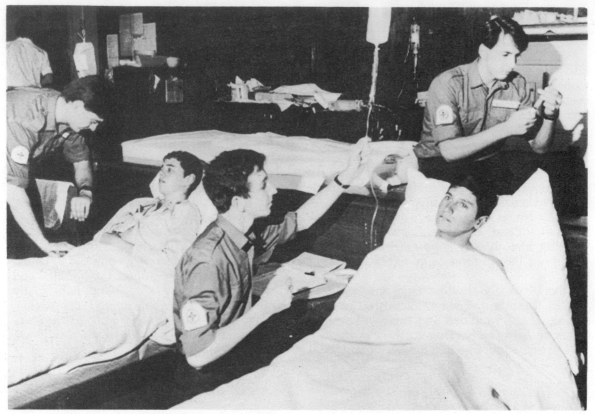

A survivor from HMS Ardent (left) shares a ward with Argentinian wounded in the hospital onboard Canberra.

important. They did not feel afraid to tell you their problems.''

Senior Nursing Officer Kidd spoke of the resilience of the wounded, how quickly they recovered and how undemanding they were.

"If they could see you were busy, they would not ask for anything. I remember how concerned they were about their friends,'' said Senior Nursing Officer Kidd.

Medical Assistant Andrew Massocchi, 25, nursed in Uganda's improvised wards. He comes from Cardiff and has vivid memories of the day badly burned Welsh Guards were brought aboard after the Sir Galahad was bombed at Fitzroy.

"There were queues of men with burns,'' he said. "Many had blackened faces and bags over their hands. They looked like mummies coming down.''

Medical assistant Massocchi said that on the voyage south he had tried to imagine what it would be like to deal with battle casualties.

"Having seen nothing like it before, I thought initially I might be rather shocked,'' he said. "But we were so busy, we did not have time to think.

"The casualties were very brave. Many of them wanted to go back to fight again.''

Medical Assistant Massocchi added: "Back here now, it seems it never happened. The memories are still there, but they are getting pushed further back in our minds.''

Surgeon Captain Roger Wilkes, a consultant general surgeon, was in charge of medical staff on board Canberra. He spoke of the very important period of training as the ship steamed south for what would be their first experience of war for many people.

The days down to the tropics and on south towards Antarctica were used to prepare the ship and the medical teams to receive wounded. Spaces were prepared to deal with each stage of a casualty's treatment, from reception and, if necessary resuscitation, to the operating theatre and the ward.

Canberra dealt with casualties immediately after the D-Day landings on May 21, but

Flying ambulance—a Royal Naval Wasp helicopter in unfamliar livery.

He likened Canberra's arrival in San Carlos to arriving in a Scottish loch. Two hours later the whole area had been transformed. It had been a shock.

Canberra was withdrawn from San Carlos to steam to South Georgia to embark units from 5th Infantry Brigade. She returned to the Falklands in cloudy weather and left after two days without incident.

Surgeon Lt.Cdr. Richard Moody, an anaesthetist at the Royal Naval Hospital, sailed in Canberra and some of her medical staff were put ashore and others transferred to Uganda. The size of her medical complement dwindled as the campaign went on.

Surgeon Captain Wilkes, who had dealt with battle casualties in Aden, said that, generally speaking, there were two sorts of casualties in the Falklands. Clean wounds on the injured from ships and field casualties with dirt, earth and other material in their wounds.

He said he had been impressed with the calm and expertise of the younger men, including the doctors, the ratings and the members of Canberra's ship's company.

A problem in the cruise ship had been large areas of armoured glass. Carpets had been taken up and hung like curtains to provide a form of protection from flying glass in the event of hits in an air attack.

"That produced a certain amount of relief, but we felt very vulnerable," said Surgeon Captain Wilkes.

He said: "If I am honest, I felt the unyielding deck of a ship was less comforting than a foxhole might have been."

Surgeon Captain Wilkes said the medical team in Canberra dealt with fit young Servicemen, who took injuries that the average young man might have taken more time to recover from.

he said one problem for the medical staff was having to share facilities with military units continuing their training on the voyage south.

He said that a night club on board had been converted into a hospital ward, with associated pantries and bars becoming sluices, a pharmacy, a pathology laboratory.

"A lot of ingenuity went into creating these spaces and running power and water into them," he said.

Surgeon Lt.Cdr. Tim Riley, from the Royal Naval Hospital, devised a ramp so that casualties could be brought straight down from the helicopter landing pad.

Surgeon Lt.Cdr. Moody stressed the importance of training on the voyage to the Falklands. Everyone had been drilled to deal with casualties in a uniform way. It had been essential preparation for dealing with large numbers of wounded.

He said an important decision had been to set up a blood bank of 1,000 units in Canberra. Troops preparing to fight had been only too willing to donate blood two weeks before the British landings.

"It was one reason why medical treatment was such a success," said Surgeon Lt.Cdr. Moody. "We always had plenty of blood. If we asked for more donors, people like the P & O crew gave blood."

A number of straightforward medical emergencies cropped up to test the system in Canberra as she headed south. The first battle casualties came on board on D-Day at San Carlos. Canberra took on board about 60 wounded that day.

"We were right in San Carlos and the air raids started at about 9 am," said Surgeon Lt.Cdr. Moody. "Casualties on their stretchers were placed on deck during the raids. A couple of times I saw medical ratings giving Argentinian wounded their own helmets.

"Everyone hit the deck and work ceased. Treatment went on as soon as the all-clear sounded. We did our operating after dark when air attacks had ceased."

Surgeons worked until about 2 am cleaning wounds, cutting away dead tissue and, following the long-standing principle of battle surgery, leaving wounds open.

Surgeon Lt.Cdr. Moody explained that wounds were not closed for five days to a week until healthy tissue was seen to be growing.

"At the end of that first night of surgery, we felt drained," he said. "We were emotionally drained. Very tired indeed."

He was later transferred to Uganda and spent two weeks on board, sometimes in the operating theatre for up to 16 hours. He returned to Canberra for the voyage home.

Looking back on the experience, Surgeon Lt.Cdr. Moody said: "We did not really learn any magical new treatments. What we did was to apply well-known principles in very difficult circumstances.

"We created our own organisation and applied well-known principles very satisfactorily. By sticking to the rules, we

Two of the Royal Navy's improvised ambulance ships—HM Ships Hydra and Herald, normally used for ocean surveying. They transported wounded from the battle zone to Montevideo.

Terra firma at last. Wounded come ashore at Montevideo redy for a flight by RAF VC10 to Brize Norton.

achieved a very successful outcome with many lives saved and many conditions minimised. By doing the right thing, we did not see all the complications."

Surgeon Lt.Cdr. Moody said his memories included the initiative and improvisation shown during the campaign. He remembered, too, the humour that was always breaking through.

Chief Medical Technician Peter Hopkins, 26, a dispenser at the Royal Naval Hospital, sailed in Uganda and received a Commendation from the Task Force Commander for his work.

It was his initial task, helped by Medical Assistant David Owen, also from the Royal Naval Hospital, to sort, index and store about 35 tons of medical supplies in Uganda.

Chief Med. Tech. Hopkins' commendation says that he worked long and arduous hours throughout the conflict. "At the height of the crisis, with casualties arriving every day, his advice and professional skills were required constantly," said the commendation.

"My over-riding memory is of the burns cases," said Chief Med. Tech. Hopkins. "They all looked the same with swollen faces. But they got better so quickly."

He added: "We were expecting there to be a lot of battle-shock casualties, but people did not seem depressed by their injuries, even when they had lost limbs. I was surprised and impressed with the way the wounded behaved."

Chief Med. Tech. Hopkins' happiest memory is of the night of May 5 when he telephoned home from Uganda to be given the news of the birth of his first child, Lucy. He was told Lucy and his wife, Mary were both fine.

That night there was a concert on board given by Royal Marines bandsmen. They marked the occasion with "Thank Heavens for Little Girls" and then "For He's a Jolly Good Fellow".

ALMIRANTE IRIZAR

For the wounded race was not relevant. British hospital ships co-operated with, and supplied equipment to the Argentine "Red Cross" ships.

BAHIO PARAISO

Guts, Professionalism, and Luck

Brigadier Julian Thompson who led 3 Commando Brigade.

The man, who led 3rd Commando Brigade to victory in the Falklands, is convinced a BBC World Service broadcast enabled the Argentinians to reinforce Goose Green before the British attacked.

Brigadier Julian Thompson, made a Companion of the Bath for his contribution to the final victory, was the man who ordered Lt.Col. H. Jones to lead 2 Para in the attack on Goose Green.

"We had expected to face the enemy on about one to one terms, but it turned out to be more like one to three in their favour," said Brig. Thompson, now a major-general.

"There is no doubt about it, the BBC World Service did report that we were going to Goose Green. Robert Fox, of the BBC, was actually with Col. Jones when they heard news of the move to Goose Green before the operation began."

Brig. Thompson said the World Service had also announced that 45 Commando was marching to Douglas Settlement and that 3 Para was going to Teal Inlet.

"So, if you like, the whole thing had been presented to them on a plate by the World Service. I don't think it was the fault of the World Service. I don't know how it happened," said Brig. Thompson.

"It was a major worry, but in the end it was not as bad as it had seemed. I am quite sure the Argentinians reinforced Goose Green because of the World Service report."

An Argentinian prisoner had told his captors of the reinforcement following the broadcast and Argentinian positions at Mount Kent had provided more proof.

"We found a lot of abandoned Argentinian slit trenches at Mount Kent," said Brig. Thompson. "Our first thought was that they had run away, but an intelligence officer established they had moved as the strategic reserve to Goose Green.

"Operational orders were found putting the unit on two hours readiness to move and they had clearly moved very quickly because they had left behind sleeping bags and other equipment."

Brig. Thompson had 2 Para under his command in 3rd Commando Brigade and on May 26, he gave Col. Jones orders to attack Goose Green. He had postponed an earlier attack because he had not been able to fly artillery forward through bad weather.

The Paras had marched to Camilla Creek house and gone to ground in barns and other buildings to hide them from enemy aircraft before they attacked the following night. It was while they lay hidden that Col. Jones heard the World Service broadcast. He was furious and dispersed his battalion immediately.

Three 105 mm light guns from 29 Commando Regiment, Royal Artillery, were flown forward by helicopter to support Col. Jones' attack on Goose Green, which had to go ahead in spite of the security breach.

"With hindsight, I wish I had put more guns there," said Brig. Thompson, who described the Paras' victory at Goose Green as a "smashing success".

He said: "I had the most enormous respect

for Col. Jones, whom I had known since he was a brigade major in Northern Ireland. I thought very highly of him. I was horrified to hear over the radio that he had been killed,—but the Paras went on and did terribly well."

Looking back to the D-Day landings on May 21, Brig. Thompson said the landings had gone very well, particularly as a full-scale rehearsal had been completely out of the question with nowhere to stage it.

The priority had been to clear the area of enemy and deploy Rapier missile units to provide anti-aircraft cover for the beach-head. Air attacks had come more quickly than expected and 3rd Commando Brigade Air Squadron had lost two Gazelle helicopters as they flew forward to clear sites for the Rapiers.

Helicopters and landing craft continued ferrying loads ashore during the air attacks and Brig. Thompson said: "By the end of the first day, we had ashore all we had expected. The main task then was to get more ammunition and fuel ashore and to begin building up for the break-out.

"Until the air battle started to swing in our favour, any attempts to re-supply people over a long period outside the air umbrella over San Carlos would have been very difficult."

Brig. Thompson, who commanded British Forces ashore until Major-General Jeremy Moore arrived a week after the landings, talked of the serious difficulties caused by the loss of the container ship Atlantic Conveyor. She had carried Chinook and Wessex helicopters.

Those helicopters were a vital part of Brig. Thompson's plans to airlift men and equipment over the appallingly difficult terrain. He was told the advance towards Port Stanley must go on, but he estimates the loss of Atlantic Conveyor and her helicopters cost him a delay of five days to a week.

"I had not anticipated half my brigade would have to walk to Port Stanley," he said.

Brig. Thompson and his staff had to begin planning for the long march—a march which was to bring the word "yomp" into everyday use—and he gave orders for the SAS to secure Mount Kent.

45 Commando and 3 Para marched east and 42 Commando was eventually airlifted to Mount Kent to hold important ground overlooking enemy positions.

With 45 Commando and 3 Para in position, Brig. Thompson was poised for the big push to take Mount Longdon, Two Sisters and Mount Harriet from the Argentinians.

"The problem was to find out where the enemy were," he said. "We had no aerial photographs and the only way we could find out what was going on was to send patrols out to go and look."

There followed ten nights of intense patrolling, with Commandos and Paras probing deep behind enemy lines to gather the intelligence vital for a co-ordinated three battalion attack.

"They were going right behind enemy lines. Some stayed behind the lines to watch and gather intelligence," said Brig. Thompson. "Sometimes, they had to fight to get out and they did it very well. The young officers and NCO's leading the patrols did a remarkable job and built up a very good picture."

The Welsh Guards' disastrous losses at Fitzroy delayed 3rd Commando Brigade's big push. Brig. Thompson held back his attack until 5 Brigade were ready. He was anxious the momentum should be maintained when the attack began.

"I thought 42 Commando would have the hardest battle because of the difficulties of the minefields around the positions they had to attack at Mount Harriet," said Brig. Thompson.

"I thought 3 Para would have the easiest task. It turned out the other way. 42 Commando had such a very good plan. They went round and attacked from the back. So much so, that they caught some of the enemy asleep.

"They had a very clever diversionary attack. The whole thing was a brilliant piece of work by 42 Commando's commanding officer, Lt.Col. Nick Vaux."

42 Commando took about 300 prisoners on Mount Harriet and Brig. Thompson said 45 Commando had a very good battle on Two Sisters, minimising their casualties by the way they "got stuck in".

3 Para had to attack head on at Mount Longdon and surprise was lost when a para triggered a mine during the silent advance under cover of darkness.

"The Paras had a very hard battle and did very well," said Brig. Thompson. "It was a difficult operation. I wanted it to be silent. If we had started with a bombardment, I knew the enemy would have retaliated with artillery.

"By being silent, I hoped the enemy would believe what they saw was just patrols."

The three-pronged assault on the mountains was a great success and was followed by British assaults on Tumbledown, Mount William and Wireless Ridge. The ground was laid for Brig. Thompson's brigade to take out Sapper Hill and go on to attack Port Stanley.

"I did not believe they would crack until we had Sapper Hill," he said. "But the morning after Tumbledown and Mount William had been taken and 2 Para, under my command, had secured Wireless Ridge, I went to see 2 Para.

"They had seen the enemy running away, harassed by our artillery."

Brig. Thompson gave orders for the brigade to advance and then heard the Argentinians had surrendered.

"My second brigade attack, for which I had given orders, never had to take place I am glad to say," said Brig. Thompson.

He walked into Port Stanley with 2 Para, but kept 45 Commando in position on Sapper Hill, backed up by artillery, in case things went wrong.

Brig. Thompson talked of the very high quality of all British troops in the campaign and of their ability to cope with very "bloody" conditions. Their training and fitness had paid off.

He said that some Argentinian units were well led and had a stiffening of good men. They had stayed and fought. Their snipers and heavy machine-guns had been a source of trouble to the British advance.

"Two things let them down," said Brig. Thompson. "Because they had troops who were not very well trained, they could not do the sort of things we could.

"This led them into the trap of believing that we could not do these things either. They tended to see us by their standards and we took them by surprise.

"They thought each of our men had a night vision device because of our performance in the dark. Their administration was bad and it was a feature of their leadership.

"They had masses of ammunition, but sometimes their soldiers went hungry. But to say they were starving is wrong and their clothing was as good as ours."

Brig. Thompson said: "We re-learned some lessons. They were lessons people knew about. I think the operation re-emphasised things we knew in our heart of hearts.

"It underlined the importance of our training to fight at night.

"The night is going to be our friend, I am convinced of that. The operation also showed the need to put a lot of fire-power at the front end of an attack."

Brig. Thompson talked of the importance of automatic weapons to bring down withering fire and of the importance of anti-tank weapons used against a dug-in enemy.

"It is quite clear you ned a lot of automatic fire at the front end to cover the gap when your own artillery and mortars have to lift to enable your troops to go forward on to enemy positions.

"We also re-learned the lesson that every time you stop you dig a hole. Even if you have to dig 10 holes in a day."

He added: "No great revelations came up, but people learned very quickly to apply lessons they had learned in their training."

Brig. Thompson praised all the units in the brigade for their work in the field and he spoke of the marvellous job done by doctors and medical staff in the improvised hospital at Ajax Bay.

Looking back on the campaign, he said: "We succeeded because of guts and professionalism and, as always, a modicum of luck. One casualty is too many, but there could have been many more."

Bandsmen in Bomb Alley

A 44-year-old Royal Marines musician from the Plymouth-based Commando Forces Band was caught on the unprotected flight deck of Canberra during an air attack on D-Day in the Falklands.

Musician George Latham was holding a rope lowering a battle casualty down a special ramp from the helicopter landing pad to the deck below.

"We had several wounded brought in by helicopter and we had got them all below except one Argentinian," said Musician Latham. "There was a big bang and I looked up and everyone was running for cover.

"There were three planes coming down San Carlos Water towards Canberra. I saw the flame from a rocket fired by one of the planes. Canberra was firing back with machine-guns.

"I was lowering the Argentinian casualty down the ramp. I wanted to get away, but I wanted to make sure the guy was all right. I had to lower him slowly and it seemed to take a long time," said Musician Latham.

"When I could see he was at the bottom, I dropped the rope and ran like hell for cover."

Musician Latham was one of the 36 musicians from the Commando Forces Band who saw service in the Falklands campaign on Canberra. They sailed in their wartime role as stretcher bearers and support teams for the Medical Squadron of Commando Logistic Regiment. By the time the campaign was over, the musicians could list over 30 tasks they had taken on.

But one of their most important contributions was to the morale of the troops preparing on Canberra to do battle for the Falklands. The musicians worked all day and then entertained at night, either playing as a complete band or in small groups.

Captain John Ware, the band's Director of music, said senior officers had described the band's effect on morale as "inestimable". Canberra's largest public room would be jampacked for the concerts and troops were eager to take part.

"When we did a concert for 40 Commando, they were all there and Brigadier Thompson, a former commanding officer of 40 Commando, came over from Fearless," said Captain Ware.

That concert was held on Canberra's midships flight deck while the ship was at Ascension Island.

"At the end of the concert, I was no longer sure who was entertaining who," said Captain Ware. "We started with the 'William Tell Overture'. There was a stunned silence to begin with and I wondered if it had been the wrong piece to play.

"But when we got to the 'Lone Ranger' bit at the end, the most almighty cheer went up. It was absolutely amazing."

As the concert progressed, the troops were invited to play percussion instruments in Latin American numbers and the baton was handed to an aspiring conductor.

"They really went to town," said Captain Ware. "At the end we had guys coming out of the audience and it became a sing-song. At the very end, we played 'Hootenanny', a selection of country and Western tunes.

The music-makers. Troops crowd Canberra's decks to hear the Royal Marines Commando Forces Band on the long voyage south. They were an important boost to morale.

"Without exception, the whole commando was on its feet. They were jumping up and down and giving each other piggy-backs. The whole deck was vibrating. It probably put the flight deck under more pressure than in the remainder of the campaign."

Captain Ware added: "Colonel Hunt, who commands 40 Commando, told me that if he could have given his men rifles and put them ashore at that moment, they would have walked right across and nothing would have stopped them."

The concert came at the end of a busy period of training and stores rationalisation at Ascension Island and the training and preparation for war continued on the voyage south to the Falklands.

The men from Commando Forces Band helped prepare Canberra to receive casualties and their many tasks included handling loads of stores airlifted on board by helicopter.

D-Day at San Carlos Water found Canberra in the thick of the air attacks after she had landed her fighting troops and begun taking battle casualties on board.

Captain Ware has a vivid memory of the beginning of that day. "It was beautiful; still, calm and clear. Imagine a calm, quiet summer dawn on Dartmoor. That is the closest I suppose you could get to it."

The calm did not last long. The Argentinians mounted savage air strikes and, miraculously, the great liner-cum-troopship came through unscathed.

Captain Ware saw Musician Latham's coolness under fire. "I saw three Mirages coming straight at Canberra, firing as they came," he said.

"We took cover, but Musician Latham stayed at his post lowering a casualty down the ramp. He went down on one knee and kept lowering the injured man. Only when the casualty was safely down did he dive for cover."

Canberra was withdrawn from San Carlos

Water that night and there was a hectic period for all on board as men, medical teams and stores were put ashore before she sailed for South Georgia.

When Canberra returned to Falkland Sound with men from 5 Infantry Brigade, cloudy weather protected her from Argentinian air strikes and she sailed after an uneventful two day stay.

The days after the Argentinian surrender on June 14 saw Canberra take on yet another role as she ferried over 4,000 prisoners-of-war from the Falklands to Puerto Madryn, Patagonia.

The Royal Marines musicians played an important part in the 28-hour non-stop operation of receiving, searching and processing the Argentinian troops. Their detailed knowledge of the layout of the huge liner was most valuable to the Guards and Paras sent on board with the prisoners.

Musicians were armed with sub-machine guns for this role—as they had been early in the campaign when they guarded wounded Argentinian special forces brought aboard.

Captain Ware said he met a number of Argentinian conscripts of mixed parentage, including one with a broad north London accent and another, who spoke English with a slight American accent. These men were used as interpreters.

Argentinian prisoners had been told Canberra had been sunk and Captain Ware recalled they were amazed to find themselves on board her heading for home.

Canberra sailed back from Patagonia to Port Stanley and the Commando Forces Band gave two concerts in the cathedral before the ship began the long voyage home.

Captain Ware said that on the last night at sea, the band Beat Retreat and played for the first time the march "San Carlos", which he had written in the South Atlantic. Captain Ware based it on "Heart of Oak" for the Royal Navy, the Paras' march "The Ride of the Valkyries" and the Commandos' march "Sarie Marais".

Everyone on Canberra seemed to have

Musicians took on many jobs—humping stores seemed to be a regular chore.

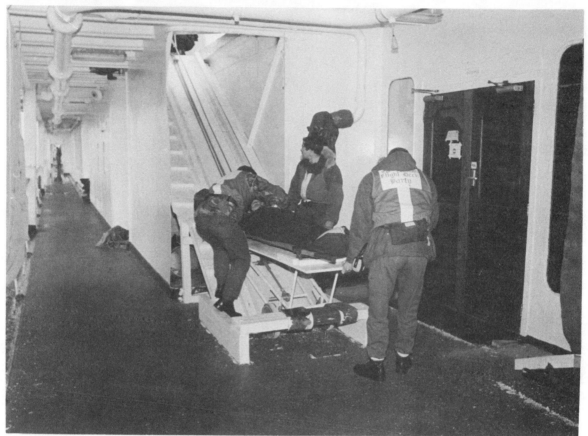

An Argentinian casualty is lowered down the ramp from Canberra's helicopter landing deck to be received by musicians from the Commando Forces Band. Yet another job . . .

found a vantage point for the final night's musical programme as the ship neared home and spectators would not let the band go after it completed Beat Retreat. It played "Hootenanny", which had become its encore number.

"It's the only time I have finished 'Beat Retreat' with that," said Captain Ware.

The band was back in action as Canberra sailed proudly up Southampton Water and "Hootenanny" was its last number as the ship neared the jetty. The Commando Forces Band then crowded to the rails with the thousands of others on board as the musicians of the Commander-in-Chief Naval Home Command's band played Canberra alongside.

Captain Ware described the campaign as a memorable experience. "One can't say one enjoyed it, but I can safely say I would not have missed it," he said.

"The band was marvellous. They proved how very useful their military role was in time of crisis and they also proved the worth of the band as a band at a time like that.

"If, at the beginning, I had been told I was going and had to choose 36 men, I don't think I could have made a better choice than the 36 men I had."

Musician Latham said he was glad to have taken part. It had not been enjoyable, but it had brought out a great spirit in the band.

"The whole thing was very unexpected for me at the end of my service; after just being in the band and then to find yourself playing soldiers," he said.

Musician Latham added: "I remember their sick faces as I lowered them down the ramp. Their faces were drained. You could not see their wounds because they were covered with blankets. But there was blood on the ramp, which had to be wiped off."

When he returned home, Musician Latham signed on for five more years with the band service and he said: "I am hoping nothing like

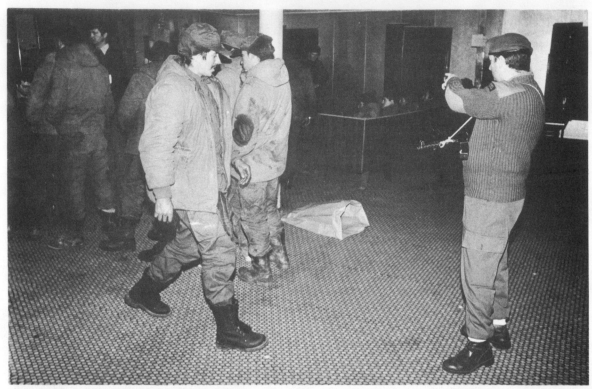

Corporal "Titch" Richardson, from Commando Forces Band, finds himself armed with a sub-machine gun to guard Argentinian prisoners on board Canberra.

Yet another job was guarding Argentinian wounded.

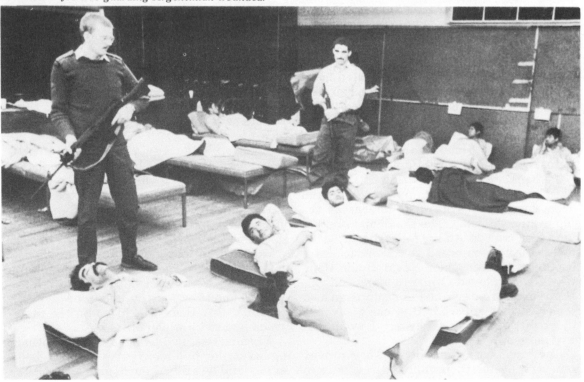

the Falklands happens again."

Sergeant Russ Ireland, 31, said: "It was an interesting experience. The greatest thing I learned was that, in a situation like that, people really got together and got on with the job.

"The guys really worked hard as a team. They worked very long hours. Often from 5 am to 8 pm and then went on to entertain the troops.

"It was the first time I had seen battle casualties. I think there was a feeling of compassion whether they were ours or theirs. There were no barriers. They needed treatment, and it was our job to get them through as quickly as possible with the least amount of pain."

Sgt. Ireland said: "It was a matter of life or death in some cases. It was a person who needed treating and the guys got on with it."

Bugler Rob Oliver, 24, helped carry casualties from the bottom of the flight deck ramp to the operating theatre.

"The Argentinian wounded seemed very young," he said. "I think they were too scared to say anything because they did not know what was going to happen to them."

He said the air strikes at San Carlos were frightening. "You did not hear the planes. Then in a split second they had come and gone. It was that fast," said Bugler Oliver.

"I remember the thuds, bangs and the screech of the planes. That was frightening. I don't think it is an experience I would like to go through again. But if it happened again, you would know what to expect."

Bombs over Brilliant

Three Argentinian bombs meant for the Devonport-based frigate, HMS Brilliant, ricochetted off the sea and bounced right over her.

That escape came on May 12 when Brilliant, the first British warship to sail for the South Atlantic, was operating close to the Falkland Islands.

She went on to escape serious damage in "bomb alley" after the British landings at San Carlos, although she was hit by cannon shells from an Argentinian jet.

Brilliant, which was accepted into service in April, 1981, had been at sea for 107 days and nights when she returned from the South Atlantic to a hero's welcome.

She was the first surface ship in the Royal Navy to break the 100 days at sea barrier since the Second World War. Her other Falklands "firsts" included being the first ship to use the Lynx helicopter and the Sea Wolf missile in action.

Captain John Coward commanded the Type 22 Frigate during the Falklands campaign and was awarded the DSO. Six of his ship's company were Mentioned in Despatches. Her laundryman, Mr Kang, from Singapore, was awarded the BEM.

Brilliant was ordered to sail from Gibraltar on March 28. Her voyage south from Ascension Island was made at breakneck speed.

She strained against the weather and came through with flying colours.

"It was beautiful," recalled Capt. Coward. "Clear blue skies, the occasional towering cumulus, but with very stiff seas and a big southerly swell. It was typical South Atlantic weather you very rarely encounter in the north.

"I think we realised for the first time what an excellent sea boat this class of ship is. We found she would go at up to 25 knots and sometimes more into the teeth of the gale.

"I remember going up to the bridge in the middle of one night and I found quite a big group of people who had just gone there to watch."

Brilliant was detached from the group of ships she was with to steam at full speed to South Georgia. Her two Lynx helicopters were much needed after two Wessex helicopters, which had been carrying SAS troops on operations in South Georgia, crashed.

As she raced to join HMS Antrim, HMS Plymouth and HMS Endurance for the operation to seize South Georgia back from the Argentinians, there was a very real threat from an Argentinian submarine known to be in the area.

"We were committed to keeping ships off the coast ready for the assault on Grytviken," said Captain Coward, "Yet we knew there was at least one submarine in the area already."

The decision was made to locate and destroy the enemy submarine and it was to play into British hands in a most unexpected way.

As Brilliant closed with South Georgia, the presence of an enemy submarine was not her only preoccupation. A number of satellite reports indicated icebergs and brash ice in the area. Brilliant could not slow her dash

HMS Brilliant, her hull pocked by cannon fire, returns proudly home to Devonport.

towards Grytviken and Captain Coward could not use radar because it would have given his ship's position away.

Her Lynx helicopters were launched at first light as she closed the coast and two hours later came the staggering news that the Argentinian submarine, Sante Fe, had been spotted on the surface leaving Grytviken.

Beside Brilliant's helicopters, Endurance, Antrim and Plymouth all had their aircraft up searching for the submarine.

"They descended on the submarine like a swarm of bees, dropping everything they had," said Captain Coward.

A Wasp helicopter dropped small depth charges, one of Brilliant's Lynx dropped a homing torpedo and the other straffed the submarine with machine-gun fire.

Sante Fe's captain had turned back for Grytviken in his stricken boat. The bridge was damaged and he was conning her through the periscope. As she beached alongside in Grytviken, her crew abandoned her and later

Brilliant's diving officer, Lt. Chris Sherman, went down to place a charge to disable the submarine further.

"The situation was suddenly different," said Captain Coward. "The submarine threat had gone. Our force was ready to go and it was decided by the Army commander that he would not wait a minute longer to go ashore.

"Then I think the most incredible and stirring moment of the whole war occurred when the ships formed a line under the towering glaciers of Grytviken and started what must have been the first British naval bombardment since World War II."

Captain Coward said: "The noise was incredible. It was multiplied because Grytviken had towering vertical mountains coming down into the sea. Every shell burst was accompanied by a hundred echoes. It must have put the fear of God into the Argentinians."

Brilliant's helicopters ferried ashore parties of SAS men, who had earlier been cross-decked to the ship. Soon the white flag was flying over Grytviken and the Argentinian commander was offering his surrender over the VHF radio.

Four days later, Brilliant sailed from South Georgia to rejoin the carrier battle group which was approaching the Total Exclusion Zone. A few days later she was detached for hush-hush operations close inshore.

May 12 saw her close to the Falklands with the Type 42 destroyer, HMS Glasgow, which had been ordered to bombard Argentinian positions around Port Stanley.

Glasgow began shelling, but the British radars soon detected enemy aircraft approaching. Brilliant positioned herself between Glasgow and the threat and prepared to fire the first Sea Wolf missiles used in a real attack.

Twelve Skyhawk jets were broken into four waves for the attack and the Sea Wolf missiles destroyed two in the first wave. A third plane crashed into the sea taking evasive action and the fourth turned away after dropping bombs and was thought to have been shot down by Argentinian fire over Port Stanley.

The second wave of Skyhawks managed to release some bombs. One went through the engine room of Glasgow. It entered the starboard side and shot out of the port side—without exploding!

Three bombs meant for Brilliant bounced over her after ricochetting off the sea. One went over the flight deck, one between her masts and once bounced over the bridge.

The bomb in Glasgow had been close to the water line, but she was escorted by Brilliant as she made her way back to the main group of ships where repairs were put in hand.

On May 19, Brilliant recovered eight SAS men, who survived when their helicopter ditched. Tragically, 21 of the crack regiment died in that crash just two days before D-Day and the British landings at San Carlos.

Lt.Cdr. Rod Morris, Brilliant's supply officer, recalled the early hours of D-Day. "When dawn came, it was a lovely day," he said. "It was sunny, calm and there were sheep grazing on the hillsides of Falkland Sound. There was an albatross wheeling nearby. It was very peaceful. Then the Argentinian planes started coming in."

It was to be a day of savage air attacks against the British ships. The Devonport-based frigate, HMS Ardent, was sunk and other ships were damaged.

When Antrim was damaged, Brilliant took over control of the defending Sea Harriers and her First Lieutenant, Lt.Cdr. Lee Hulme, directed the British planes in many successful engagements.

Captain Coward moved from a position in Falkland Sound into the neck of the anchorage to improve close in air cover.

"This had two effects," he said. "It improved our air defence of the anchorage, but it put my radar in the shadow of the land, which was only a matter of yards away.

"We had not, at that stage, developed techniques that were successful later for using Sea Wolf under those conditions. We fell back on Bofors and machine-guns as our principle means of protection."

Captain Coward said it became clear the Argentinians could not keep up the pace of their vicious air attacks for long.

"By coming in at sea level, they were giving themselves some protection from the hills and rocks until the last minute. But they were denying themselves the ability to select their targets properly and to launch their bombs from the right height," said Capt. Coward.

A Mirage jet attacked Brilliant with cannon fire and shells swept up her starboard side. One shell penetrated the operations room and three men had to be transferred to the hospital ship Uganda with slight injuries.

Some electrical compartments were damaged, but Capt. Coward said his engineers managed to get the systems working again by nightfall.

"One shell took out the officers' heads," said Lt.Cdr. Morris, who quipped: "It was one of the most underhand moves the enemy could make."

He added: "Another shell caused severe damage to the wine and spirit stocks in the wardroom."

Brilliant left "bomb alley" on May 25 to rejoin the carrier group. It was Argentine's national day and a day for massed air attacks on the British ships. Broadsword, Brilliant's sister-ship, was hit, the destroyer HMS Coventry, was sunk and the container ship Atlantic Conveyor was hit by an Exocet missile.

Lt.Cdr. Morris recalled seeing the Atlantic Conveyor soon after she was crippled and said she was a "great mass of black smoke". The container ship was about 4½ miles from Brilliant and the warship picked up 24 survivors.

Lt.Cdr. Morris explained that Brilliant had been "goal-keeping" for HMS Invincible at the time. It meant she aimed to be in a position between the carrier and an incoming missile during any attack and shoot down the missile with her Sea Wolf.

He believed Brilliant would have shot down the Exocet if it had come towards his ship and not gone some miles ahead into the unfortunate Atlantic Conveyor.

"Some of the Atlantic Conveyor's older men were very cold and very shocked," said Lt.Cdr. Morris. "But one of her officers had a survival suit on. He came into our wardroom, unzipped the suit, stepped out in full Merchant Navy uniform and asked when the bar opened."

From then until the Argentinian surrender on June 14, Brilliant was engaged in convoy duties before she started the 8,000 miles voyage home.

Lt.Cdr. Morris said his lasting impression was the feeling of pride in the way the ship's company performed.

"The average age was 19 to 20 and there is nothing special about them in terms of where they come from or their background. They are a good cross-section of British youth and they were fantastic."

Captain Coward said the campaign had been a fine vindication of Brilliant's design.

"The ship's company demonstrated the thoroughness of modern naval training," he said. "I had no worries about any of them at any time. If they had any worries, they certainly never showed them."

Behind enemy lines

Rigid raiding craft from Devonport probed deep behind Argentinian lines on cloak and dagger operations with special forces during the battle for the Falklands.

Royal Marines from the 1st Raiding Squadron sometimes spent several days behind the lines, operating at night and then laying-up by day in carefully camouflaged positions.

They used what scant cover was available in the bleak landscape. Seaweed might be piled over their raiding craft to hide them from prying eyes and the men would go to ground for the daylight hours in thick tussock grass.

They could not afford to leave any tell-tale signs for Argentinian patrols or for enemy helicopters, which might chance on their positions.

Working with the SAS and the Special Boat Squadron on raids and intelligence gathering missions was only one of the 1st Raiding Squadron's many roles in the South Atlantic.

The 17ft rigid raiding craft proved ideal for many tasks and became maids of all work in the Falklands. Their 140 hp outboard engines give them a top speed of about 30 knots.

They worked with Commando and Parachute Regiment units, ferrying men, munitions and stores. They landed patrols and ambush teams, evacuated casualties and provided a vital water-borne "taxi service".

Captain Chris Baxter, who commanded the squadron, took 31 men with him, leaving behind an important back-up party, all dis-appointed to have missed the action in the Falklands. Down to the Falklands went 17 rigid raiding craft and a further 17 inflatable Geminis, which the squadron did not use.

Four of the Geminis were loaned to the Commando Logistic Regiment and one was used to move an unexploded bomb from the logistic landing ship, Sir Lancelot, which was hit during one of the many air attacks.

Most of the 1st Raiding Squadron were brought hastily back from Arctic warfare training in Norway to join the Task Force and they had little time before they sailed south in RFA Sir Galahad.

It was the squadron's first operational deployment and Captain Baxter said: "The campaign gave us a new lease of life. The operation could not have been done without raiding craft. We have new terms of reference and new equipment. The campaign was good for us."

The squadron had a busy time at Ascension Island on the way to the Falklands, but it was only a taste of what lay ahead. The rigid raiding craft were in the thick of the campaign from D-Day when the British troops went ashore at San Carlos.

The squadron's little craft operated throughout the frequent air attacks and Lance-Corporal Philip Vrettos, said his most vivid memory was of San Carlos on D-Day.

"Those air raids when we were out alone in our boats were a new thing and quite terrifying. We got caught in a lot of bombing raids," said Lance-Corporal Vrettos.

Captain Baxter talked of the dangers from

the air attacks and he recalled the day Marine "Knocker" White had a lucky escape during the attack on the Ajax Bay hospital. Two bombs fell near Marine White's raiding craft, but neither exploded.

Bombs were not the only hazard. Squadron boats were strafed on a number of occasions as Argentinian planes swooped low over San Carlos.

As the campaign progressed, Captain Baxter found himself with a couple of craft at his base at San Carlos and the rest of his squadron scattered far and wide with a number of units.

Shortly after the D-Day landings, Lance-Corporal Vrettos and another member of the squadron went on operations with special forces.

"We set up a base on an island and we used it to lay up during the day," said Lance-Corporal Vrettos.

Tussock grass gave them cover, but they found to their disgust that the island was infested with rats, which ate rations and found their way into clothing and equipment. The operation continued until after 2 Para had won the battle for Goose Green.

Navigating at night in poorly charted waters was made even more difficult by frequent mist or drizzle.

"At night, if the visibility was bad, we had to play a lot of it by ear," said Lance-Corporal Vrettos. "It was very eerie at first to be operating behind enemy lines, but, after a while, we began to accept it as normal.

"I enjoyed working with the special forces. I suppose it is what the squadron was designed for in the first place."

Lance-Corporal Nigel Smith was on board Sir Galahad when she was hit while landing the Welsh Guards at Fitzroy. The move to the logistic landing ship had come as a pleasant change.

"It was like a rest to us," said Lance-Corporal Smith. "We had been working nonstop. We were able to have our first shower in a couple of weeks on board Galahad."

He had been summoned to Galahad's

Lance Corporal Philip Vrettos (left), Marine Barry Gilbert (centre), and Lance Corporal Nigel Smith of 1st Raiding Squadron saw plenty of action during the campaign in their tiny craft.

bridge and was talking to the captain when the Argentinian planes attacked. He had been in Sir Lancelot when she was hit and he knew only too well the sound of the bombs being released.

"We hit the deck," he recalled. "We felt the whole ship lifted up under us. We tried to get down from the bridge, but we could not. There was a dead man on the deck behind the bridge. We tried to get down, but there was thick black smoke.

"We ended up climbing over the front of the bridge and down a crane to the deck."

Lance-Corporal Smith asked another man to help him heave five-gallon petrol tanks from the two rigid raiders over the side to prevent them exploding in the blaze that was engulfing Sir Galahad. Ammunition was exploding and there was no way off the deck.

When he moved up to the bow, Lance-Corporal Smith saw men coming up from below with "horrendous" burns.

"We could not get below to help. Men were coming up in a hell of a state," said Lance-Corporal Smith. "There were about 40 of us on the bow and we were stuck. Then the chopper pilots started coming in. They were fantastic.

"They took off the badly injured, mainly Chinese. We tried to get the liferafts over the side. We could not get them in and, when we did, they capsized. We got one upright and some of the men got into it. There were about 20 of us left and we thought the whole ship was going to explode."

Lance-Corporal Smith and the others were eventually taken off by a Mexeflote and he later flew back to HMS Fearless. He had been shot at during air attacks earlier in the campaign, but he said Galahad stuck in his mind more than anything else.

"I was lucky to get off Galahad alive," he said. "You did not know what was going to happen until you got ashore. It was pretty horrendous. You felt so helpless. You wanted to do something but there was nothing you could do."

Just before the Argentinian surrender, Marine Barry Gilbert and three other members of the squadron, Sgt Buckley and Marines Kavanagh and Nordass, were sent on special operations close to Port Stanley.

Their rigid raiding craft were taken in close by boat and the men hid for the next day on a tiny island, covering their craft with seaweed and lying-up in tussock grass.

"We waited for the signal for the raid to go ahead and then left under cover of darkness to rendezvous with special forces," said Marine Gilbert.

There was a close brush with an Argentinian ship blazing with lights on the run in to the rendezvous. Marine Nordass remained at the pick-up point as the rest of the party left for the raid.

"There was a lot of fire from another action nearby and we found ourselves floodlit by flares at one point as we approached the landing beach for the raid," said Marine Gilbert.

"We landed the special forces, but they came under heavy fire as they went forward. They were forced to withdraw. I had stayed with the boat on the beach. More flares went up as we withdrew.

"I went straight towards an Argentinian ship, zig-zagging at full speed and still under fire from machine-guns. I headed into the cover of the ship and around behind it," said Marine Gilbert.

"I was just trying to work out a way to get clear. By then, it looked like mortar fire was coming down on our original rendezvous."

The rigid raiders were all abandoned and their coxswains and the special forces, including three wounded, made their way to a pre-arranged rendezvous well away from the beaches. The wounded were evacuated by helicopters from 3rd Commando Brigade Air Squadron.

"We laid up that night and very early the next morning we saw the white flags over Port Stanley," said Marine Gilbert, who was Mentioned in Despatches for his part in the operation.

Captain Baxter said that Sgt Buckley's craft had been damaged and he had limped away from the scene to put his party ashore further along the coast to make their way to the rendezvous in the hills.

Marine Nordass, waiting with his craft at the original pick-up point, had to abandon it when he came under fire.

Captain Baxter said: "The scope of the Falklands operation provided an excellent opportunity for the squadron to show its potential. The coxswains and their craft were extended far beyond their normal experience.

"In the main they acquitted themselves extremely well, showing a high degree of personal skill and craft serviceability. Many lessons were learned as a result. I think they did marvellously well."

Five rigid raiding craft were lost, four in the raid with special forces and one on Sir Galahad, but the squadron escaped with only one minor injury.

On the lighter side, Marine "Bungy' Williams showed typical resourcefulness in bagging Upland geese and hare with a shotgun.

"We were able to trade them for sausages, eggs and other good things from the ships," recalled Captain Baxter.

1st Raiding Squadron gained one recruit in the Falklands, but he decided the military life was not for him.

Marine Philip Owen explained that a penguin, found covered in oil on the beach at San Carlos, had quickly been adopted by the squadron.

"We washed him off and fed him with pusser's pilchards" said Marine Owen. "We put him in a box after a slight drop of whisky to warm him up.

"We christened him Marine Galtieri and the sergeant-major inspected him and told him to get his hair cut. Next day, we took him to the water to see if he would swim. He did a runner and disappeared."

Marine Owen said: "The campaign was something I would not like to do again, but I would if I had to.

"My birthday was on June 15, the day after the Argentinians surrendered. Just knowing the war was over was the biggest present I could have had."

Problems and Successes

Rear-Admiral Robert Gerken, Flag Officer 2nd Flotilla. Many of his ships sailed south to battle.

The lack of airborne early warning radar and sophisticated weapons systems hampered when ships had to fight very close to land were just two of the problems faced by the Task Force according to Rear-Admiral Robert Gerken, Flag Officer 2nd Flotilla.

Many ships from his flotilla sailed south and he talked of some of the problems and successes of the Falklands operation; of his admiration for the performance of his ships and men; and of his belief that some changes should be made in the light of the Falklands experience.

"I am personally very much campaigning for some modifications to ships in the light of experience," said Admiral Gerken. "These modifications would be to the weapons fit, but that is all I can say."

One modification he was prepared to discuss was to the Type 22 frigates, currently armed with Exocet and Sea Wolf missiles, torpedo tubes and a Lynx anti-submarine helicopter.

"I would very much hope as we go on building more of the Type 22's that we will see a modification to mount a gun of the Mark 8 type. I could see it being done easily by mounting it forward of the bridge and moving the Exocet launchers further aft. There is now a lighter and more compact launcher for the Exocet, which was not available when we were designing the Type 22's."

Naval guns had a vital part to play, not only in air defence, but in bombarding shore targets. Type 21 frigates from Devonport's "Fighting-Fourth" Frigate Squadron gave a considerable amount of gunfire support.

Their shells pounded targets during "feint" attacks and in attacks on Argentinian positions before the British landings.

Admiral Gerken said that some of the spotting was done by members of the Special Air Service and Special Boat Service, who had been quietly slipped ashore.

He said the 4.5 inch naval gun was accurate to within 100 yards on its first shot and then very quickly hit the target through corrections from spotters. It could be directed along a line of trenches with great accuracy and was used against aircraft, fuel dumps, anti-aircraft missile sites, gun positions and other important targets.

"Ships were engaged night after night in attacks on the Argentinian positions to the west of Port Stanley," said Admiral Gerken. "They contributed to the seizing of each of the pieces of high ground.

"They fired thousands of rounds, which, with the Royal Artillery bombardments, brought down such a fire that it must have had a very significant effect on the Argentinian will to fight for Port Stanley.

"It came as not too much of a surprise that, as they gradually fell back in the face of the combined bombardment, their will to take on our forces was steadily broken."

Admiral Gerken said that Broadsword and Brilliant and Type 42 destroyers had been very much used as forward radar direction platforms to detect enemy aircraft and guide British Harriers into attack positions.

"It meant putting them forward and put-

The picture that says it all. Major-General Moore immediately after the surrender was signed at Stanley.

ting them at risk," he said. "But you risk a less important unit to safeguard your major units. Had we suffered significant damage which put out of action either of our carriers, the course of the campaign could have been dramatically affected."

Admiral Gerken said controllers in the Type 22's and Type 42's radioed information from ships' radars to Harrier pilots. Sheffield was attacked and lost while involved in the task.

Admiral Gerken talked of the difficulties over the years of maintaining a balanced capability to fight both on and under the sea. He said a significant decision had been not to build a new class of Fleet carriers with airborne early warning radar, surface attack and air defence capability and a fixed-wing anti-submarine capability.

Hermes and Invincible had provided the Task Force with air defence aircraft, but they were not backed up by airborne early warning

radar to detect low-flying enemy planes and enable our combat air patrols to attack the enemy before they came within range of our ships or forces ashore.

He said that the Sea Wolf missiles carried in Broadsword and Brilliant had been "wrong footed" on some occasions in the early stages of the operation by hostile aircraft weaving in their attack run.

The control computer, in a system designed for near "hands off" control, had, on occasions, to be over-ridden.

"It was the first time we had the opportunity to use Sea Wolf against real enemy aircraft," said Admiral Gerken. "We had success both with the radar mode and in the visually-aimed mode with a man taking charge. We destroyed five aircraft with Sea Wolf."

Admiral Gerken spoke of the difficulties the ships faced in waters close to land when attacking aircraft used the land to cover their approach.

Antelope and Ardent were both sunk while close to shore giving air defence cover to the amphibious landing fleet.

"The fact that Argentinian attacks were directed against the warships on the outer perimeter of defence and other warships were hit, was a measure of the defence they provided," said Admiral Gerken.

"They soaked up a very large number of bombs and near misses. One might surmise that, if they had not been taken by Royal Navy units, more would have gone into the ships that were landing Royal Marines and Paras and all their supporting units."

Admiral Gerken explained that British ships had to maintain constant vigilance for Argentinian submarines, particularly the two German-built Type 209's commissioned in 1974.

"The threat was very great indeed," he said. "Particularly once our approach to the Falklands was going to have to be made with a large number of amphibious and supporting merchant ships. It meant the enemy was going to be able to identify focal points we would have to pass and position his submarines to attack us.

"We mounted a continuous and comprehensive anti-submarine warfare operation. We had to assume they were putting themselves in the worst position as far as we were concerned."

Admiral Gerken said that submarine-like contacts and sightings of what could have been periscopes were investigated and mortars, torpedoes and depth charges were used against what were considered to be submarine-like contacts in the vicinity of our forces. He had no confirmation of any damage to any submarine.

He said that Type 21 frigates were used on special operations by crack troops from the SAS and SBS, who were put ashore on vital intelligence gathering missions and to mount attacks against Argentinian positions.

Admiral Gerken had a special pat on the

Argentinian POW's tramp past one of their wrecked Pucarra aircraft at Stanley airport.

back for the radio operators, many of them still in their teens, who quickly and accurately dealt with a vast flow of signal traffic during the operation.

He talked of the make do and mend spirit and of the way ships helped each other with spares. Resourceful artificers and mechanicians had found their own ways to solve problems far from home.

He referred to the support the fighting ships received from merchant vessels taken up from trade for the operation and of the front-line support given by oil-rig support vessels in maintenance and repairs.

"The people involved gained immensely from the pressure they worked under, from the successes and from the reverses that came their way," said Admiral Gerken.

"From what I heard from the captains, the men in the ships surpassed anything that could possibly have been thought of their capability."

He talked of their endurance and continuing sharpness over long periods on watch; of the endurance of upper deck gun crews in extreme cold; of personal bravery under fire or in coping with fires and flooding in damaged ships.

"What we look upon as a naval tradition was very, very well borne out by their performance and their great humour, which kept breaking through," said Admiral Gerken.

He recalled the captain who jokingly said to a young seaman when the going was particularly bad "We have all got to go sometime". The youngster replied "You're all right. You've had half your life. I've only just started mine".

Admiral Gerken said: "We are a better navy. It is only by taking on something like this operation that the priorities suddenly get put in the right order."

"One of the great worries of the men down there was how their families were at home," said Admiral Gerken. "War is 90 per cent boredom and 10 per cent terror. They knew what degree of danger they were in, but they worried about how worried their families would be. That was their main worry."

Campaign memories

Argentine POWs wait in the streets of Stanley to be called forward for embarkation and the voyage home.

The mess they left behind . . . Men of the Task Force were amazed at the state of Stanley when they marched in. The pile of discarded weapons beside the road to Stanley Airfield.

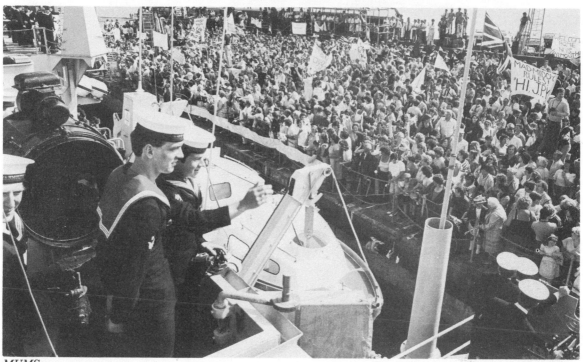

MUMS...
A typical scene at every homecoming... Here men of HMS Yarmouth are amazed at their reception at Rosyth. The boys had sailed... The men were back...

& MEDALS...
Lt Col Nick Vaux proudly displays his DSO.

THE FAMILIES RETURN

Almost a year after the fighting families of those lost in the campaign returned to the islands, on board the luxury liner Cunard Countess, to pay their final respects.

The War Graves at Blue Beach, San Carlos are dedicated. VIP's and families from the UK witness the moving ceremony. Falkland Islanders joined them in their grief.

We will remember.....

The men of the Task Force
who died in the South Atlantic.

Lt.Col. H. Jones, shortly before landing in the Falklands.

Private Richard Absolon
Petty Officer Michael Adcock
Air Eng Mech Adrian Anslow
Mne Eng Mech Frank Armes
Able Seaman Derek Armstrong
Rifleman Raymond Armstrong
Sergeant John Arthy
WO2 Malcolm Atkinson
Staff Sgt John Baker
Lt Commander David Balfour
Lt Commander Richard Banfield
Able Seaman Andrew Barr
Lieutenant James Barry
Lt Commander Gordon Batt
Corporal William Begley
L/Corporal Gary Bingley
Able Seaman Ian Boldy
Petty Officer David Briggs
Petty Officer Peter Brouard
Private Gerald Bull
L/Corporal Barry Bullers
Corporal Paul Bunker
L/Corporal Anthony Burke
Corporal Robert Burns
Private Jason Burt
Chief Petty Officer John Caddy
Marine Paul Callan
Mne Eng Art Paul Callus
L/Sergeant James Carlyle
Petty Officer Kevin Casey
Bo'sun Chee Yu Sik
L/Corporal Simon Cockton
Private Albert Connett
Catering Assistant Darryl Cope
L/Corporal Anthony Cork
Private Jonathan Crow
Sergeant Philip Currass
Lieutenant William Curtis
Guardsman Ian Dale
Sergeant Sid Davidson
Marine Colin Davison
A/Petty Officer Stephen Dawson
Guardsman Derek Denholm
Captain Christopher Dent

Elect Fitter Dis Leung Chau
Private Stephen Dixon
A/Wpns Eng Mech John Dobson
Private Mark Dodsworth
Cook Richard Dunkerley
Guardsman Michael Dunphy
Butcher Dis Sung Yuk Fai
Cook Brian Easton
Sergeant Clifford Elley
Sub Lieutenant Richard Emly
Sergeant Roger Enefer
Sergeant Andrew Evans
Corporal Kenneth Evans
Guardsman Peter Edwards
Chief Petty Officer Anthony Eggington
Lt Commander John Eyton-Jones
Petty Officer Robert Fagan
L/Corporal Ian Farrell
C/Sergeant Gordon Findlay
Corporal Peter Fitton
Chief Petty Officer Edmund Flanagan
Private Mark Fletcher
A/Ldg Cook Michael Foote
Mar Eng Mech Stephen Ford
Major Michael Forge
Petty Officer Michael Fowler
Lieutenant Kenneth Francis
WO2 Laurence Gallagher
Sapper Pradeep Gandhi
Guardsman Mark Gibby
Guardsman Glenn Grace
Guardsman Paul Green
Private Anthony Greenwood
L/Corporal Brett Giffen
Cook Nigel Goodall
S/Sergeant Christopher Griffen
Marine Robert Griffin
Guardsman Gareth Griffiths
Private Neil Grose
3rd Eng Officer Christopher Hailwood
Wpns Eng Mech Ian Hall
Captain Gavin Hamilton
A/Steward Shaun Hanson
Corporal David Hardman

Corporal William Hatton
Flt Lieutenant Garth Hawkins
Able Seaman Sean Hayward
Lieutenant Rodney Heath
Air Eng Mech Mark Henderson
2nd Eng Officer Paul Henry
Able Seaman Stephen Heyes
L/Corporal Peter Higgs
Air Eng Mech Brian Hinge
Chief Radio Officer Ronald Hoole
Corporal Stephen Hope
Guardsman Denis Hughes
Guardsman Gareth Hughes
Sergeant William Hughes
A/Sergeant Ian Hunt
Private Peter Hedicker
Private Stephen Illingsworth
Mne Eng Art Alexander James
Guardsman Brian Jasper
Private Timothy Jenkins
C/Sergeant Brian Johnston
Sapper Christopher Jones
Private Craig Jones
Private Michael Jones
Lieut Colonel Herbert Jones
Corporal Philip Jones
Sailor Kam Yung Shui
Guardsman Anthony Keeble
L/Sergeant Kevin Keoghane
Laundryman Lai Chi Keung
Laundryman Kyo Ben Kwo
Ldg Mne Eng Mech Allan Knowles
Private Stewart Laing
Wpns Eng Mech Simon Lawson
Chief Petty Officer David Lee
Sergeant Robert Leeming
Marine Eng Mech Alistair Leighton
L/Corporal Paul Lightfoot
Corporal Michael Love
L/Corporal Christopher Lovett
Corporal Douglas MacCormack
Marine Gordon Macpherson
Cook Brian Malcolm
Guardsman David Malcolmson

Guardsman Michael Marks
Naval Airman Brian Marsden
Ldg. Cook Tony Marshall
Marine Stephen McAndrews
Corporal Keith McCarthy
Air Eng Art Kelvin McCullum
Corporal Michael McHugh
Sergeant Ian McKay
L/Corporal Peter McKay
Corporal Stewart McLaughlin
Corporal Andrew McIlvenny
Air Eng Mech Allan McAuley
Private Thomas Mechan
Corporal Michael Melia
Private Richard Middlewick
A/Ldg Mne Mech David Miller
L/Sergeant Clark Mitchell
Guardsman Christopher Mordecai
3rd Eng Off Andrew Morris
A/Ldg Seaman Michael Mullen
L/Corporal James Murdoch
Lieutenant Brian Murphy
Ldg P.T. Inst Gary Nelson
L/Corporal Stephen Newbury
Corporal John Newton
Guardsman Gareth Nicholson
Petty Officer Anthony Norman
Marine Michael Nowak
Lieut Richard Nunn
Major Roger Nutbeam
Staff Sgt Patrick O'Connor
Cook David Osborne
A/Wpns Eng Mech David Ozbirn
A/Petty Officer Andrew Palmer
Private David Parr
Guardsman Colin Parsons
L/Corporal John Pashley
Mne Eng Mech Terence Perkins
Guardsman Eirwyn Phillips
Marine Keith Phillips
Seaman Po Ng
Guardsman Gareth Poole
Staff Sergeant James Prescott
Private Kenneth Preston
Corporal Stephen Prior
L/Air Eng Mech Donald Pryce
Guardsman James Reynolds
Cook John Roberts
Lt Commander Glen Robinson-Moltke
Craftsman Mark Rollins
Sergeant Ronald Rotherham
Guardsman Nigel Rowberry
Marine Anthony Rundle
L/Cook Mark Sambles
L/Corporal David Scott
Private Ian Scrivens
Lt Commander John Sephton
Craftsman Alexander Shaw
Seaman Shing Chan Chai
L/Cook Anthony Sillence
Sergeant John Simeon
Private Francis Slough

Corporal Jeremy Smith
Private Mark Holman-Smith
L/Corporal Nigel Smith
Corporal Ian Spencer
L/Radio Op Bernard Still
Guardsman Archibald Stirling
Able Seaman Matthew Stuart
Steward Mark Stephens
Mar Eng Art Geoffrey Stockwell
L/Corporal Anthony Streatfield
Steward John Stroud
Chief Petty Officer Kevin Sullivan
Cook Andrew Swallow
L/Corporal Philip Sweet
A/Weap Eng Art David Strickland
Able Seaman Adrian Sunderland
Corporal Paul Sullivan
Corporal Stephen Sykes
Sapper Wayne Tabard
Guardsman Ronald Tanbini
L/Corporal Christopher Thomas
Guardsman Glyn Thomas
L/Corporal Nicholas Thomas
Guardsman Raymond Thomas
Chief Petty Officer Michael Till
Lieutenant David Tinker
Mne Eng Mech Stephen Tonkin
A/Cook Ian Turnbull
Corporal Andrew Uren
Petty Officer Colin Vickers
Corporal Laurence Watts
Guardsman James Weaver
Guardsman Andrew Walker
Petty Officer Barry Wallis
Corporal Edward Walpole
L/Corporal Christopher Ward
WO2 Daniel Wight
A/Ldg Marine Eng Mech Garry Whitford
Master at Arms Brian Welsh
Ldg Cook Andrian Wellstead
Private Philip West
Sergeant Malcolm Wigley
A/Wea Eng Art Philip White
A/Ldg Mar Eng Mech Stephen White
Guardsman David Williams
Mne Eng Mech Gilbert Williams
Apprentice Ian Williams
Cook Kevin Williams
Marine David Wilson
Corporal Scott Wilson
Captain David Wood
Lt Commander John Woodhead

MERCHANT NAVY
Captain Ian North
John Dobson
Frank Foulkes
James Hughes
David Hawkins
Ernest Vickers